Spectacularity of Designs

OrangeBooks Publication

1st Floor, Rajhans Arcade, Mall Road, Kohka, Bhilai, Chhattisgarh - 490020

Website:**www.orangebooks.in**

© Copyright, 2024, Author

All rights reserved. No part of this book may be reproduced, stored in a retrieval system, or transmitted, in any form by any means, electronic, mechanical, magnetic, optical, chemical, manual, photocopying, recording or otherwise, without the prior written consent of its writer.

First Edition, 2024

ISBN: 978-93-5621-829-1

SPECTACULARITY OF DESIGNS

THE CANVAS OF TOMORROW: UNVEILING NEW HORIZONS

AR. RAHUL MEHTA

OrangeBooks Publication
www.orangebooks.in

A Book For The New Age Architects and Interior Designers Who Like to Think Out of The Box

As, we gaze into the crystal ball of the future, we see a world of endless possibilities and untapped potential, waiting to be shaped and molded by the hands of visionaries and dreamers. The future of the design industry is a tapestry of trends and directions, woven together by the threads of creativity, innovation, and sustainability.

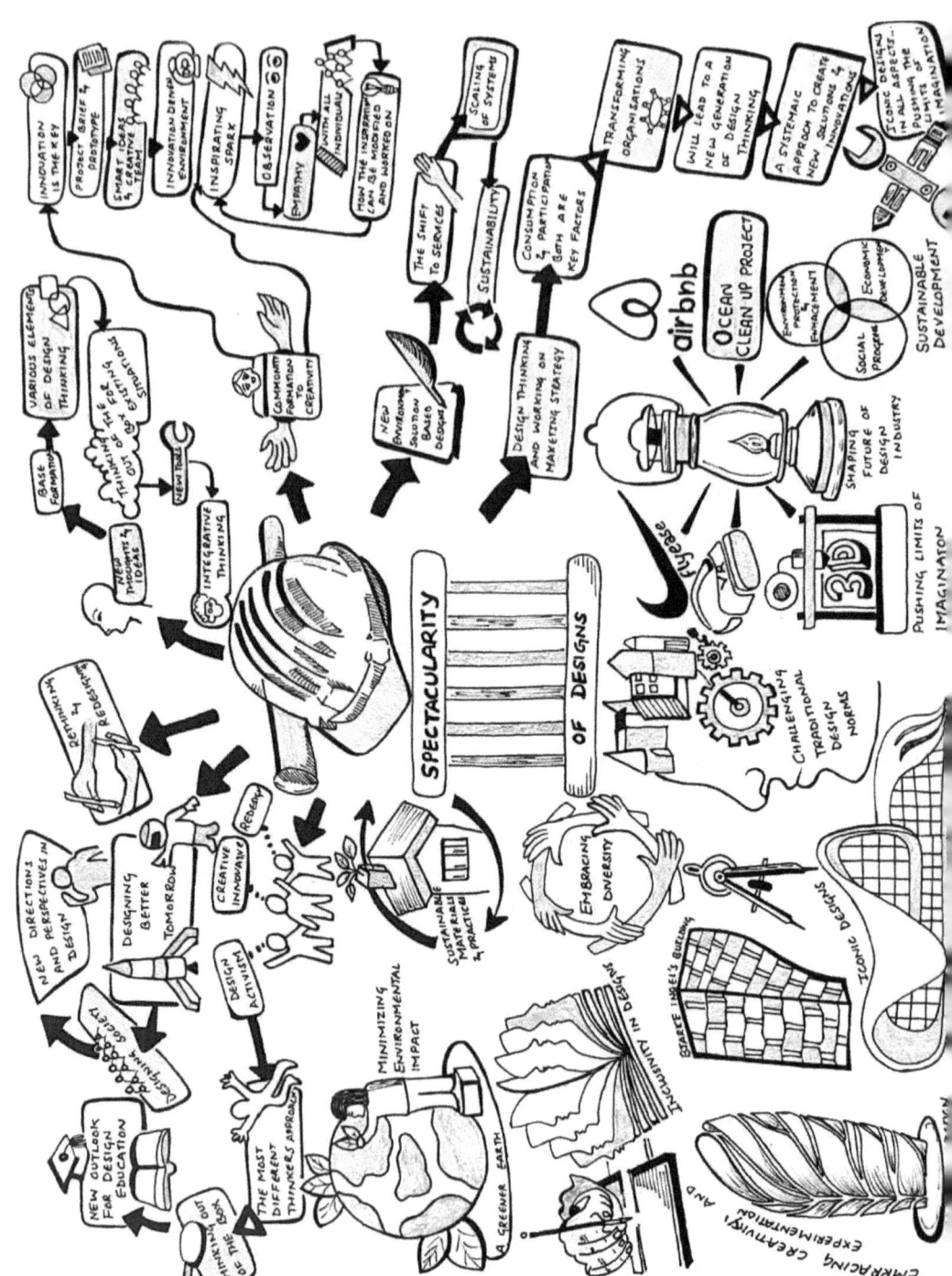

Preface

In the dazzling design world, where creativity knows no bounds and innovation reigns supreme, we find ourselves immersed in a realm of infinite possibilities and boundless imagination. Design has the power (the line should start from here which I am not able to backspace that) to enrich our lives and shape our surroundings in spectacular ways. From the structures we inhabit to the objects we interact with daily; design touches every aspect of the human experience. Welcome to "Spectacularity of Designs" a journey to explore the spectacular nature of design through various lenses, showcasing innovative approaches, integrating technology with aesthetics, challenging norms, and pushing the boundaries of imagination.

In this book, we embark on a captivating odyssey through fifteen chapters, each offering a unique perspective on the extraordinary spectrum of design. From the iconic landmarks that define our skylines to the innovative solutions that redefine our everyday experiences, we delve deep into the heart of design to uncover its awe-inspiring beauty and transformative power.

This collection's chapters showcase the best modern design thinking and practice. We begin by exploring what makes designs "spectacular" and the elements that elevate designs to the realm of the extraordinary. Innovative design approaches utilizing emerging technologies are discussed to demonstrate how designers push the boundaries of what is possible. The integration of aesthetics and technology in spectacular designs is examined through contemporary examples.

The book also challenges traditional norms in design and argues for more experimental and boundary pushing approaches. The author has discussed how designers can shape the future of the industry by embracing new materials, techniques, and ideas. Creativity and imagination are championed as key drivers of spectacular designs. The importance of balancing form and function through thoughtful design is emphasized.

The later chapters celebrate the cultural and human elements of design. We explore how diversity, inclusivity, and cultural influences can inspire spectacular designs. The book also promotes eco-friendly and sustainable design practices through examples of designs that minimize environmental impact through material choices and production methods.

Overall, the chapters in this collection argue that what makes designs "spectacular" goes beyond just aesthetics it is the combination of thoughtful innovation, human relevance, technological integration, and positive impact that truly elevates designs and turns them into something extraordinary.

As we embark on this journey through the "Spectacularity of Designs," let us be inspired by the creativity, innovation, and passion that define the design world. From the grandest architectural marvels to the smallest everyday objects, let us celebrate the beauty and ingenuity of designs that shape our world and inspire us to dream bigger, reach higher, and create a future filled with endless possibilities. This book hopes to encourage readers to see design in a new light, appreciate its spectacularity, and envision what the future of this creative discipline could hold. Great designs have the power to spark joy, promote progress, and change the world for the better. I hope this book will inspire designers and design enthusiasts to push their creativity and imagination to create the spectacular designs of tomorrow.

Ar. Rahul Mehta

Acknowledgments

Writing a book is never a solitary endeavor, and thinking out of the box is like painting on The Canvas of Tomorrow for Unveiling New Horizons. I would like to express my deepest gratitude to all those who have contributed their time, expertise, and support to make this project possible.

First and foremost, I am immensely grateful to the visionary designers, innovators, and thought leaders whose work has inspired the content of this book. Your creativity, passion, and dedication to architecture and design have served as a guiding light throughout the writing process.

I am also indebted to the numerous organizations, institutions, and companies resources, data, and case studies are used in the book to explain the concepts in a better way. Your contributions have helped to illustrate the real world impact of architecture and design and have brought the midframe to see the concepts discussed in this book.

I would like to acknowledge the support of my family members, friends, and colleagues who have encouraged and cheered me on throughout the writing process. I would like to thank especially my mother **Mrs. Anil Bala Mehta** for being the torch bearer and motivator of all times. Your words of encouragement, constructive feedback, and unwavering belief in me have been invaluable. I would also like to thank my father, **Mr. Rohit Mehta**, for his steadfast support and silent strength. Your quiet confidence in my abilities has provided me with a sense of stability and reassurance. To my siblings, thank you for your understanding and patience during the working hours I spent engrossed in writing. Your support and love have been a source of comfort and inspiration. I am deeply grateful for my Wife's help, patience, and understanding throughout this process. Your unwavering faith in my abilities has been a source of inspiration and confidence. I am profoundly grateful for your patience and understanding as I dedicated countless hours to this project. My heartfelt thanks also go to my extended family, whose encouragement and faith in my vision have meant the world to me. Your kind words and unwavering support have been invaluable. I would like to acknowledge my friends, who have been my cheerleaders and critical sounding boards. Your insightful feedback, late night brainstorming sessions, and genuine support have significantly contributed to the completion of this book.

I extend my sincere gratitude to OrangeBooks Publication and their entire team for their invaluable support and expertise in bringing this book to life. Your dedication and professionalism have been truly exceptional.

Finally, I would like to express my deepest gratitude to the readers of this book. It is my sincere hope that the ideas and insights presented in these pages will inspire you to rethink your approach to design and to become agents of positive change in the world. To all of you, thank you from the bottom of my heart. Your support has made this endeavor possible, and I am profoundly grateful for each and every one of you. Thank you all for your contributions, support, and commitment to building a more sustainable and equitable future through design.

With all my love and gratitude,
Ar. Rahul Mehta

Contents

Preface .... *vii*

Acknowledgments .... *ix*

1. Exploring the Spectacularity of Designs 1
2. Innovative Approaches in Modern Design 8
3. Integration of Technology and Aesthetics 18
4. Challenging Traditional Design Norms 25
5. Shaping the Future of Design Industry 30
6. Embracing Creativity and Experimentation 36
7. Redefining the Boundaries of Design 44
8. Pushing the limits of Imagination 53
9. Balancing form and function 61
10. Embracing Diversity in Design 68
11. Celebrating Cultural Influences 75
12. Promoting Inclusivity in Design Practices 83
13. Championing Eco-Friendly Designs 94
14. Sustainable Materials and Practices 102
15. Minimizing Environmental Impact 117

1
Exploring the Spectacularity of Designs

Design is more than mere aesthetics; it is a profound expression of creativity, functionality, and cultural significance. "Exploring the Spectacularity of Designs" investigates the awe-inspiring world of design, uncovering the elements that make certain creations stand out as truly spectacular. This chapter examines the intersection of form, function, and innovation, highlighting how exceptional designs capture our imagination, shape our experiences, and reflect the zeitgeist of their times. From iconic architectural marvels to groundbreaking products and visionary digital interfaces, we will explore what makes these designs not only visually striking but also deeply impactful. Join us on a journey through the spectacular, where each design tells a story, and every detail holds the potential to inspire and transform. In the arts, film directors usually associate special visual effects, such as the representation of ghosts, with the use of the color green, the human body, and actors, to the increased representation of the Ethereal Body. Designers and developers, when trying to adapt new technologies and other concepts to everyday life objects to bring to life experiences, do not choose these two paths.

Imagine a world where chess pieces talk to each other, a holographic image tells the story of the place of its birth, or a sculpture reacts positively or negatively to the touch of human hands. In a world like this, the pieces of the chess game that already presided over a draw, with the pieces passing information to each other, would surely, a short time later, leave the chess board and walk to where the other objects that also presented the spectral life are. They are objects designed to offer an interactive experience to the users. The manifestation of the spectrum in design is not often investigated, but innumerable are the opportunities to apply the concepts presented herein (which are related to the classification of the spectrum through the meaning of life, the act of communication, and knowledge) in the development of artworks able to extrapolate the normal form of fundamental interaction between user and object.

1.1 Introduction to The Concept of Design and Its Significance

Designing is a primary mission of every human society to create innovative/more performing artifacts to support its modernity, functionality, and aspirations. It involves visualizing, illustrating, and creating artifacts across disciplines to meet human needs, aspirations, and desirability. Speculative actions, these representations can be attributed to absent or abstract artifacts that provide users with a design and expressive tool for materializing them. Behind every significant operation or set of operations involved in any design activity, a point of view of the importance of this operation is a principal motivator. This point of view is the aspect of the design which includes the surrounding process of the designing, extraction, and manipulation of the resulting artifacts through either the use or the reuse of it, the act of creation, and the creation itself.

Designing has the intentionality to create artifacts which are fit for intended functions and uses. Its earliest start can be dated back to the prehistoric era, but unassertively, design has an implicit status among the primitive and in the alphabetic era of human society. In cipher designing, it became more explicit during the Renaissance around the 15th and 16th centuries when para-artist architects, e.g., Leonardo da Vinci (1452-1519 BC), started to view their artifacts as solutions to mathematically and scientifically expressed problems of their ages. Since then, modern designing, as the Renaissance product, through modernity and post modernity, to the current era, has moved from a relatively art chasen phase through engineering or science chasen phases, to the current design methodology, i.e., a blend of both artistic and engineering/scientific engagements towards humancentric emphasis. This chapter aims to delve into the precise reasons why these iconic forms are so captivating, often without the need for explanation or commentary. Each of these characteristics indicates or is derived from (or both) the scientific basis behind the effectiveness of iconic design aesthetics and our unique human attraction to these qualities. We derived fundamental answers for both from the Mind, Brain, and Education Sciences, which deepen our understanding of designing to meet the needs of the individual and to be more empathetic about how designs will be perceived and utilized. Whether from common products or brand experiences, we can improve the effectiveness of our designs by cultivating the principles of iconic design and understanding why the prevailing sensory, narrative, and audience characteristics of other iconic designs captivate our attention.

Over time, designers have crafted visual symbols with enduring traits of simplicity and accessibility, strong ties to their surroundings, layouts hinting at spatial order, and memorable emotional qualities that attract users and audiences. These qualities allow these symbols to transcend language and cultural barriers, thereby allowing them to deliver their messages to broad audiences. The visual symbols, including, but not limited to, national flags, corporate identifiers, or animated characters, are ubiquitous.

(a) Innovative Concepts

Every design idea starts with innovativeness of the designer and his/her perspective of seeing things. These "simplification for elegance" approaches are the guiding aesthetics of many designs of most representative designers. Any true innovation is complex and takes the thinking of the designer to another level In other words, the rules of proportion about beauty, simplicity, clarity, and craftsmanship only apply when you go to solve a known problem, and for a solution to resonate with us emotionally, and empathetically. We also need to work with strikingly different requirements: the necessity of scientific accuracy, anthropomorphism, or the elephant in the room. Iconic designers of the latest designs embody a different set of qualities that are described as three reasons why their work is so fused by each other, and they are guided by a pursuit of distinctive, innovative, clear, and distinct features.

Not all of the design concepts we have been taught in school about proportion and color apply to iconic designs. Many of the iconic designers out there did not even plan to invent a chair, a lamp, or a home. They were more likely to address a specific problem which may be a day-to-day problem or a problem that is lingering through ages. When Simon Berry and Ben Belton designed the Afripipes Water Roller, they were thinking about how to solve the problem of carrying drinking water to their families. They might have been thinking in interesting ways about how a barrel would roll more easily than it could be lifted, or they might have realized that the kids in their families would be more likely to roll an empty barrel to the nearest open well rather than carrying it.

1.2 Examples of Iconic Designs Across Different Fields

Iconic designs are those that transcend their immediate function to become cultural touchstones, admired and revered across generations. They are the pinnacle of creativity, innovation, and craftsmanship, representing the highest achievements in their respective fields. From architecture and fashion to product design and beyond, iconic designs captivate our imaginations and leave an indelible mark on the world.

(a) Architecture

In the realm of architecture, certain buildings stand out as iconic symbols of human achievement and ingenuity. One such example is the Sydney Opera House in Australia, designed by Danish architect Jørn Utzon. Completed in 1973, the Sydney Opera House is renowned for its striking sail like roof structure and sculptural form, which have made it one of the most recognizable landmarks in the world. The building's innovative design and engineering solutions, including the use of precast concrete shells, revolutionized the field of architecture and earned it UNESCO World Heritage status in 2007.

Another additional iconic architectural design is the Guggenheim Museum Bilbao in Spain, designed by architect Frank Gehry. Opened in 1997, the museum is celebrated for its organic, sculptural form and use of titanium panels, which shimmer in the sunlight and reflect the surrounding landscape. The Guggenheim Bilbao has become a symbol of urban revitalization and cultural renaissance, drawing millions of visitors each year to its exhibitions and events.

(b) Fashion

In the world of fashion, certain designs transcend trends and become timeless classics that continue to inspire and influence designers and consumers alike. One such example is the little black dress, famously popularized by French fashion designer Coco Chanel in the 1920s. Simple, elegant, and versatile, the little black dress is a staple of women's wardrobes around the world, symbolizing sophistication and effortless style.

Another additional iconic fashion design is the Alexander McQueen "bumster" trousers, created by British fashion designer Alexander McQueen in the 1990s. Characterized by their low rise waistline and provocative silhouette, the bumster trousers challenged traditional notions of proportion and fit, pushing the boundaries of fashion and sparking debate about body image and gender norms.

(c) Product Design

In the real domain of product design, certain creations stand out for their innovative features, elegant aesthetics, and enduring appeal. One such example is the iPhone, introduced by Apple Inc. in 2007. Combining cutting edge technology with sleek design aesthetics, the iPhone revolutionized the smartphone industry and transformed the way we communicate, work, and play. With its intuitive interface, seamless integration of hardware and software, and iconic minimalist design, the iPhone has become a cultural icon and a symbol of innovation and progress in the digital age.

Another iconic product design is the Tesla Model S, introduced by Tesla, Inc. in 2012. As the world's first premium all electric sedan, the Model S challenged conventional notions of automotive design and performance, offering zero emission driving without compromising on style or luxury. With its sleek, aerodynamic silhouette, cutting edge electric propulsion system, and advanced autopilot features, the Model S has redefined the automotive industry and inspired a new generation of electric vehicles.

(d) Graphic Design

In the realm of graphic design, certain creations stand out for their visual impact, creativity, and effectiveness in communicating messages and ideas. One such example is the "I Love NY" logo, created by graphic designer Milton Glaser in 1977. With its simple, bold design and iconic heart symbol, the "I Love NY" logo has become a global symbol of love, unity, and solidarity, transcending its original purpose as a tourism promotion campaign to become a cultural phenomenon.

Another iconic graphic design is the NASA "worm" logo, introduced by the National Aeronautics and Space Administration in 1975. Designed by Richard Danne and Bruce Blackburn, the "worm" logo is celebrated for its minimalist, futuristic aesthetic and symbolic representation of NASA's mission to explore the cosmos. With its sleek, stylized letterforms and distinctive red chevron, the "worm" logo has become synonymous with space exploration and scientific discovery.

In conclusion, iconic designs across different fields share common traits of innovation, elegance, and timeless appeal. Whether it's a landmark building, a fashion masterpiece, a revolutionary product, or a memorable logo, these designs have the power to captivate our imaginations, inspire our creativity, and shape our collective identity. By celebrating and studying iconic designs, we gain valuable insights into the principles and practices that drive excellence in design and innovation.

1.3 Analysis of What Makes These Designs Stand Out and Captivate Audiences

What sets iconic designs apart from their counterparts is their ability to capture the imagination and evoke an emotional response from audiences. Whether it's the awe-inspiring beauty of a landmark building, the timeless elegance of a fashion masterpiece, or the innovative functionality of a groundbreaking product, these designs have a certain magic that captivates and inspires.

At the heart of every iconic design is a combination of innovation, functionality, and aesthetic appeal. These designs push the boundaries of what is possible, challenging conventions and redefining standards of excellence in their respective fields. They embody the spirit of creativity and ingenuity, pushing the envelope and breaking new ground in pursuit of perfection.

Innovation is perhaps the most crucial element of iconic designs. Whether it's a groundbreaking new technology, a revolutionary construction technique, or a novel approach to materials and aesthetics, innovation drives progress and sets these designs apart from the rest. Iconic designs are not content to simply follow trends; they seek to create them, pushing the limits of what is possible and redefining the possibilities of their respective fields.

Functionality is another key factor in the success of iconic designs. While aesthetics may initially capture the attention of audiences, it is the functionality of a design that ultimately determines its long term success. Iconic designs seamlessly blend form and function, prioritizing usability, accessibility, and user experience without sacrificing style or elegance. They are designed with the needs of the end user in mind, anticipating their desires and exceeding their expectations at every turn.

Aesthetic appeal is perhaps the most subjective aspect of design, yet it is also one of the most powerful. Iconic designs have a certain visual allure that transcends cultural boundaries and speaks to audiences on a universal level. Whether it's the graceful curves of a building, the intricate detailing of a garment, or the sleek lines of a product, these designs possess a timeless beauty that resonates with people from all walks of life.

In conclusion, iconic designs are the result of a perfect storm of innovation, functionality, and aesthetic appeal. They are the products of creative genius and tireless dedication, capturing the imagination and inspiring awe in all who encounter them. Detailed analysis of what makes these designs stand out and captivate audiences, we can gain valuable insights into the principles and practices that drive success in the world of design.

2

Innovative Approaches in Modern Design

Innovation is the lifeblood of design, a relentless force that pushes the boundaries of what is possible and challenges conventional wisdom at every turn. In this chapter, we journey through the dynamic and ever evolving landscape of modern design. We will explore recent trends reshaping the industry, innovative solutions addressing both old and new challenges, and the transformative impact of technology on the creative process. By understanding how cutting edge advancements are integrated into design, we gain insight into how designers are revolutionizing their field. This chapter highlights the ingenuity driving contemporary design and illuminates the potential for future breakthroughs that promise to redefine our interaction with the world. Through this exploration, we will see how innovation, fueled by creativity and technology, continues to elevate design to new heights, making it an indispensable tool for progress and improvement in every facet of life.

2.1 Recent Trends and Innovations in Design

Design is a dynamic field, constantly evolving to meet the changing needs and desires of society. In this chapter, we will explore the latest trends and innovations that are shaping the world of design today. From sustainable practices to digital advancements, designers are embracing new approaches to create impactful and meaningful solutions.

(e) The Rise of Sustainability

In recent years, sustainability has emerged as a central theme in design, driven by growing concerns about environmental degradation and climate change. Designers are increasingly incorporating eco-friendly materials, renewable energy sources, and sustainable practices into their projects, with a focus on reducing waste, minimizing carbon emissions, and preserving natural resources.

One trend that has gained traction is the use of recycled and upcycled materials in design. From furniture made from reclaimed wood to clothing crafted from recycled plastic bottles, designers are finding innovative ways to repurpose materials and give them new life. By embracing the principles of the circular economy, designers can create products that are not only beautiful and functional but also environmentally responsible.

Another trend is the adoption of biophilic design principles, which seek to reconnect people with nature in the built environment. Biophilic design incorporates elements such as natural light, greenery, and natural materials into indoor spaces, creating environments that promote health, wellbeing, and productivity. From living walls to daylighting strategies, designers are harnessing the power of nature to create spaces that inspire and rejuvenate.

(f) Digital Transformation

Advances in digital technology have revolutionized the design process, providing designers with powerful tools and techniques to bring their ideas to life. One trend that has emerged is the use of parametric design software, which allows designers to generate complex, organic forms using algorithms and computational tools. Parametric design enables designers to explore a virtually infinite range of design possibilities, from intricate facades to dynamic interiors.

Not able trend is the integration of virtual reality (VR) and augmented reality (AR) technologies into the design process. VR and AR allow designers to create immersive, interactive, and responsive environments that blur the line between physical and digital space. From virtual walkthroughs to interactive digital installations, designers are using VR and AR to engage users in new and exciting ways.

Additionally, 3D printing technology has revolutionized the way products are designed and manufactured. With 3D printing, designers can create custom objects with unprecedented precision and efficiency, eliminating the need for traditional manufacturing processes. From custom jewelry to personalized prosthetics, 3D printing offers endless possibilities for customization and innovation.

(g) *HumanCentered Design*

At the heart of design is the desire to create solutions that improve the lives of people. HumanCentered design, also known as user centered design, is an approach that prioritizes the needs, preferences, and experiences of users throughout the design process. By involving end users in the design process from the outset, designers can create products, services, and experiences that are truly user centric.

One trend in humancentered design is the emphasis on inclusivity and accessibility. Designers are increasingly designing products and environments that are accessible to people of all ages, abilities, and backgrounds. From inclusive playgrounds to adaptive clothing, designers are finding innovative ways to make the world more inclusive and welcoming for everyone.

Another trend is the use of co-design and participatory design methods, which involve collaborating with end users to co-create solutions that meet their needs and preferences. By involving end users in the design process, designers can gain valuable insights and feedback that inform the design process and ensure that the final product meets the needs of its intended users.

The world of design is constantly evolving, driven by a desire to create solutions that are both innovative and impactful. From sustainability to digital transformation to humancentered design, designers are embracing new approaches to address the challenges and opportunities of the 21st century. By staying attuned to the latest trends and innovations, designers can continue to push the boundaries of creativity and create solutions that make a positive difference in the world.

2.2 Case Studies Highlighting Innovative Design Solutions

Innovation in design is not just about creating something new; it's about solving complex problems, improving lives, and leaving a lasting impact on society. In this chapter, we will explore several case studies that exemplify the power of innovative design solutions across various industries and domains. From urban revitalization to environmental conservation to user centric innovation, these case studies showcase how designers are pushing the boundaries of creativity and making a difference in the world.

(a) Case Study 1: The High Line, New York City
The High Line is perhaps one of the most iconic examples of urban revitalization through innovative design. Once a dilapidated elevated railway track running through Manhattan's West Side, the High Line has been transformed into a vibrant public park and green space that has captured the imagination of millions of visitors from around the world.

Conceived by landscape architects James Corner Field Operations and Diller Scofidio + Renfro, the High Line project sought to repurpose the disused railway infrastructure into a public amenity that celebrates the history of the site while providing much needed green space in the heart of the city. The design team faced numerous challenges, including navigating complex zoning regulations, securing funding, and engaging with local communities.

The design solution was both innovative and inspired. The High Line features a meandering pathway that winds its way through a lush landscape of native plants, wildflowers, and grasses, interspersed with seating areas, art installations, and gathering spaces. The elevated vantage point offers sweeping views of the city skyline, creating a unique and immersive experience for visitors.

One of the key innovations of the High Line project is its approach to sustainability. The park incorporates green infrastructure elements such as rain gardens, permeable paving, and sustainable drainage systems to manage stormwater runoff and reduce the urban heat island effect. Native plant species were selected for their resilience and ability to thrive in the harsh urban environment, creating habitat for birds, insects, and other wildlife.

The High Line has become a beloved community asset that has revitalized the surrounding neighborhood, attracting millions of visitors each year and generating economic activity for local businesses. Beyond its role as a public park, the High Line has inspired similar projects in cities around the world, demonstrating the power of innovative design to transform neglected urban spaces into vibrant, thriving community hubs.

(b) Case Study 2: The Ocean Cleanup Project

Plastic pollution is one of the most pressing environmental challenges of our time, with millions of tons of plastic waste entering the world's oceans each year. The Ocean Cleanup Project is a groundbreaking initiative that seeks to address this problem through innovative design solutions.

Founded by Dutch inventor Boyan Slat in 2013, the Ocean Cleanup Project developed a revolutionary system to collect plastic debris from the ocean using passive floating barriers and currents. The system, known as the Ocean Cleanup Array, consists of large floating barriers that harness ocean currents to passively capture plastic debris while allowing marine life to pass through unharmed.

The collected plastic is then recycled and repurposed into new products, reducing the environmental impact of plastic pollution on marine ecosystems. The Ocean Cleanup Project has conducted extensive research and testing to refine the design of the Ocean Cleanup Array, deploying prototypes in the Great Pacific Garbage Patch and other oceanic gyres to evaluate their effectiveness.

The key innovative parts of the Ocean Cleanup Project is its focus on scalability and efficiency. By leveraging the power of ocean currents to passively collect plastic debris, the Ocean Cleanup Array can cover large areas of the ocean with minimal energy input. The system is designed to be modular and adaptable, allowing it to be deployed in a variety of oceanic conditions and locations.

The Ocean Cleanup Project has the potential to clean up millions of tons of plastic waste from the world's oceans, helping to protect marine life, conserve natural resources, and mitigate the impacts of plastic pollution on the environment. Through its innovative design solutions, the Ocean

Cleanup Project is paving the way for a cleaner, healthier ocean for future generations.

(c) Case Study 3: Airbnb's Design Thinking Approach

Airbnb is a global online marketplace that connects travelers with unique accommodations around the world. One of the keys to Airbnb's success is its innovative design thinking approach, which prioritizes user experience, empathy, and creativity in the design process.

Through extensive user research, prototyping, and iterative testing, Airbnb has created a platform that is intuitive, user friendly, and highly engaging for both hosts and guests. From the visual design of the website and app to the layout of listings and search functionality, every aspect of the Airbnb experience is carefully crafted to delight users and enhance their travel experience.

Airbnb's design thinking approach is its emphasis on inclusivity and accessibility makes it unique. The platform is designed to be accessible to people of all ages, abilities, and backgrounds, with features such as built in translation, accessibility filters, and user generated content that reflects the diversity of Airbnb's global community. Another innovation is Airbnb's focus on community building and social connection. Through features such as host profiles, guest reviews, and social events, Airbnb fosters a sense of belonging and community among its users, encouraging them to connect and share their experiences. By embracing a design thinking approach, Airbnb has revolutionized the way people travel and experience the world, providing a platform that empowers individuals to connect with new cultures, communities, and experiences in a meaningful and authentic way. Through its innovative design solutions, Airbnb has transformed the travel industry and inspired millions of people to explore the world in new and exciting ways.

(d) Case Study 4: Solar Impulse 2

Solar Impulse 2 is a solar powered aircraft that made history by completing the first round the world flight powered solely by solar energy. Designed and piloted by Swiss aviators Bertrand Piccard and André Borschberg, Solar Impulse 2 demonstrated the potential of renewable energy and clean technology to revolutionize aviation and reduce carbon emissions.

The aircraft's innovative design features a wingspan longer than a Boeing 747, covered in over 17,000 solar cells that power four electric motors and lithium-ion batteries. By harnessing the energy of the sun, Solar Impulse 2 was able to fly day and night without the need for traditional fossil fuels, completing its epic journey across four continents and three oceans.

Through its groundbreaking design and technology, Solar Impulse 2 has inspired a new generation of innovators and entrepreneurs to explore sustainable alternatives to traditional aviation, paving the way for a cleaner, greener future for air travel. The project has demonstrated the potential of renewable energy to revolutionize transportation and reduce greenhouse gas emissions, highlighting the importance of innovation and creativity in addressing the challenges of climate change.

These case studies highlight the transformative power of innovative design solutions to address complex challenges and create positive change in the world. From urban revitalization to environmental conservation to user centric innovation, designers are harnessing their creativity, ingenuity, and passion to make a meaningful impact on society, industry, and the environment. Embracing innovation and pushing the boundaries of what is possible, designers can continue to create solutions that improve lives, inspire change, and shape a better future for generations to come.

2.3 Exploration of How Technology Has Influenced and Propelled Design Forward

In the world of design, technology has emerged as a powerful catalyst for innovation, creativity, and progress. From digital tools to advanced materials to sustainable manufacturing processes, technology has revolutionized the way designers conceptualize, create, and interact with the world around them. In this chapter, we will explore how technology has influenced and propelled design forward, shaping the future of the discipline in profound and transformative ways.

(a) Digital Tools and Software

One of the most significant ways technology has influenced design is through the development of digital tools and software. Computer aided design (CAD) software allows designers to create detailed 2D and 3D models of their ideas, enabling them to visualize concepts, iterate on designs, and communicate their vision with clients and collaborators more effectively than ever before.

Furthermore, advancements in virtual reality (VR) and augmented reality (AR) technology have opened up new possibilities for immersive and interactive design experiences. Designers can now create virtual environments that allow users to experience their designs in 3D, providing valuable insights into spatial relationships, scale, and proportion. Additionally, cloud based collaboration platforms enable designers to work together in real time, regardless of their geographic location. These tools facilitate seamless communication and collaboration, streamlining the design process and fostering creativity and innovation.

(b) Advanced Materials and Manufacturing Processes

Technology has also revolutionized the materials and manufacturing processes available to designers. Advances in materials science have led to the development of new materials with unique properties and capabilities, opening up new avenues for creativity and experimentation.

For example, 3D printing technology allows designers to create complex geometries and intricate structures that would be impossible to achieve using traditional manufacturing methods. From custom furniture to wearable art, 3D printing offers endless possibilities for innovation and customization. Similarly, digital fabrication techniques such as laser cutting, CNC machining, and robotic manufacturing enable designers to produce highly precise and detailed objects with minimal waste. These processes are revolutionizing the way products are designed and manufactured, making it easier and more cost effective to bring ideas to life. Furthermore, sustainable manufacturing processes such as additive manufacturing and bio-fabrication offer promising alternatives to traditional manufacturing methods, reducing the environmental impact of production and promoting a more sustainable approach to design.

(c) Internet of Things (IoT) and Smart Design

The Internet of Things (IoT) has transformed the way we interact with the objects and environments around us, paving the way for a new era of smart design. By embedding sensors, actuators, and connectivity into everyday objects, designers can create products and spaces that are responsive, adaptive, and intelligent.

For example, smart home devices such as thermostats, lighting systems, and security cameras can be controlled remotely via smartphone apps, allowing users to monitor and adjust their home environment from anywhere in the world. Similarly, wearable technology such as fitness trackers and smartwatches can provide real time feedback on health and wellness metrics, empowering users to make informed decisions about their lifestyle and behavior.

In the realm of urban design, IoT enabled smart cities are leveraging technology to improve efficiency, sustainability, and quality of life for residents. From intelligent transportation systems to energy efficient buildings to connected infrastructure, smart cities are harnessing the power of data and connectivity to create more livable, resilient, and equitable communities.

(d) Artificial Intelligence (AI) and Machine Learning

Artificial intelligence (AI) and machine learning are revolutionizing the design process, enabling designers to automate repetitive tasks, generate creative ideas, and analyze complex datasets with unprecedented speed and accuracy.

For example, generative design algorithms use AI and machine learning to explore thousands of design options and identify the most optimal solutions based on predefined criteria such as performance, cost, and sustainability. These tools empower designers to explore new design possibilities and push the boundaries of creativity and innovation. Similarly, AI powered design assistants can provide valuable insights and recommendations to designers throughout the design process, helping them make more informed decisions and optimize their workflows. From concept generation to material selection to prototyping, AI is revolutionizing every aspect of the design process.

Technology has fundamentally transformed the practice of design, enabling designers to push the boundaries of creativity, innovation, and sustainability in unimaginable ways. From digital tools and advanced materials to smart design and artificial intelligence, technology has become an indispensable tool for designers seeking to create meaningful and impactful solutions to the challenges of the 21st century. Embracing technology and harnessing its power enables designers to continue propelling the field of design forward, shaping the future of the discipline, and improving lives around the world. With innovative tools and digital advancements at their disposal, designers can explore new creative horizons, enhance their problem solving capabilities, and develop solutions that address complex global challenges. This integration of technology not only drives the evolution of design but also fosters a more interconnected and adaptive world, where creativity and innovation lead to tangible improvements in everyday life.

3
Integration of Technology and Aesthetics

In the contemporary landscape of design, the convergence of technology and aesthetics has become increasingly prevalent, ushering in a new era of innovation and creativity. This chapter explores how technology and aesthetics intertwine to shape modern design practices, from digital art to interactive installations to smart environments. We delve into how designers leverage technology to enhance the aesthetic appeal of their creations, pushing the boundaries of what is possible and redefining the relationship between form and function.

3.1 Examination of How Technology Has Transformed the Aesthetics of Design

In the ever evolving landscape of design, technology has played a pivotal role in reshaping aesthetics, offering new avenues for creativity, expression, and innovation. This chapter delves into the profound impact of technology on the aesthetics of design, exploring how digital tools, materials, and processes have revolutionized the way designers conceptualize, create, and experience aesthetic beauty.

(a) The Evolution of Aesthetics in Design

Aesthetics, the study of beauty and taste, has long been a central concern in design. From the classical proportions of ancient architecture to the intricate ornamentation of Baroque art to the sleek minimalism of modern design, aesthetic preferences have evolved, reflecting changes in culture, technology, and society.

With the advent of digital technology, the boundaries of aesthetics in design have expanded exponentially. Digital tools such as computer aided design (CAD), parametric modeling, and digital rendering have democratized the design process, allowing designers to explore a virtually infinite range of aesthetic possibilities with unprecedented speed and precision.

(b) Digital Tools and Visualizations

One of the most significant ways technology has transformed the aesthetics of design is through the proliferation of digital tools and visualizations. CAD software, for example, enables designers to create highly detailed 2D and 3D models of their designs, allowing them to experiment with form, proportion, and scale in ways that were previously impossible.

Digital rendering techniques further enhance the visual representation of designs, enabling designers to create photorealistic images and animations that accurately simulate materials, textures, and lighting conditions. These digital visualizations not only facilitate communication and collaboration among designers, clients, and stakeholders but also allow designers to explore different aesthetic options and iterate on their designs more efficiently.

(c) Parametric Design and Algorithmic Aesthetics

Parametric design, a computational approach to design that uses algorithms to generate form and structure, has revolutionized the aesthetics of design by enabling designers to create complex, organic geometries that respond to specific parameters and constraints. By harnessing the power of algorithms, designers can explore a wide range of aesthetic possibilities and generate designs that are highly optimized for performance, efficiency, and aesthetics.

Algorithmic aesthetics, the study of beauty in computational systems, has emerged as a new frontier in design, challenging traditional notions of aesthetics and creativity. From generative algorithms that create intricate patterns and textures to evolutionary algorithms that optimize designs based on predefined criteria, algorithmic aesthetics offer new ways of thinking about beauty and form in the digital age.

(d) Digital Fabrication and Material Exploration
Advancements in digital fabrication technologies such as 3D printing, laser cutting, and CNC machining have revolutionized the way designers approach materiality and construction. These technologies enable designers to create highly customized and intricate forms with unprecedented precision and efficiency, opening up new possibilities for aesthetic expression.

Digital fabrication also facilitates material exploration, allowing designers to experiment with a wide range of materials, finishes, and textures to achieve the desired aesthetic effect. From lightweight composite materials to bio based polymers to digital ceramics, designers can now choose from a vast palette of materials to create designs that are not only beautiful but also sustainable and environmentally friendly.

Technology has fundamentally transformed the aesthetics of design, offering new tools, materials, and processes that have revolutionized the way designers conceive, create, and experience aesthetic beauty. From digital tools and visualizations to parametric design and algorithmic aesthetics to digital fabrication and material exploration, technology has expanded the boundaries of aesthetics in design, opening new possibilities for creativity, expression, and innovation.

As technology continues to evolve and advance, the aesthetics of design will continue to evolve with it, pushing the boundaries of what is possible and redefining our understanding of beauty in the digital age. By embracing technology and harnessing its power, designers can continue to push the boundaries of creativity and create designs that inspire, delight, and resonate with audiences around the world.

3.2 Examples of Cutting Edge Technologies Used in Design Processes

Advancements in technology continue to push the boundaries of what is possible in design, enabling designers to explore new frontiers of creativity, efficiency, and innovation. This part of the chapter showcases cutting edge technologies revolutionizing the design process, from virtual reality to artificial intelligence to additive manufacturing. Through these examples, explore how technology reshapes how designers conceive, create, and bring their ideas to life.

(a) Virtual reality (VR) and augmented reality (AR)

Virtual reality (VR) and augmented reality (AR) are immersive technologies that enable designers to visualize and interact with their designs in 3D, providing a more intuitive and immersive design experience. VR allows designers to immerse themselves in virtual environments and explore their designs from every angle, providing valuable insights into spatial relationships, scale, and proportion.

AR, on the other hand, overlays digital information onto the physical world, enabling designers to superimpose virtual models onto real world environments and visualize how their designs will look and function in context. These technologies are particularly useful for architects, interior designers, and urban planners, allowing them to create immersive and interactive experiences that engage clients and stakeholders in the design process.

(b) Generative Design and Computational Design

Generative design and computational design are computational approaches to design that use algorithms to generate and optimize form and structure based on predefined criteria and constraints. These technologies enable designers to explore a vast range of design options and identify the most optimal solutions based on performance, efficiency, and aesthetics.

Generative design algorithms use evolutionary algorithms, genetic algorithms, and other computational techniques to explore thousands of design possibilities and identify the most promising solutions. These algorithms can optimize designs for specific criteria such as weight, material usage, and structural integrity, resulting in highly efficient and optimized designs.

Computational design, on the other hand, uses algorithms to create complex geometries and patterns that respond to specific parameters and constraints. These algorithms enable designers to create intricate and organic forms that would be impossible to achieve using traditional design methods, opening up new possibilities for aesthetic expression and innovation.

(c) Additive Manufacturing (3D Printing)
Additive manufacturing, also known as 3D printing, is a revolutionary manufacturing process that enables designers to create complex and customized objects with unprecedented precision and efficiency. Unlike traditional manufacturing methods, which involve subtracting material from a solid block, additive manufacturing builds objects layer by layer from digital models, allowing for greater design freedom and flexibility.

3D printing technology is used across a wide range of industries, from aerospace and automotive to healthcare and fashion, enabling designers to create everything from prototypes and custom components to finished products and architectural elements. The ability to create highly customized and complex geometries has revolutionized the way designers approach materiality, construction, and fabrication, opening up new possibilities for creativity and innovation.

(d) Artificial Intelligence (AI) and Machine Learning
Artificial intelligence (AI) and machine learning are revolutionizing the design process, enabling designers to automate repetitive tasks, generate creative ideas, and analyze complex datasets with unprecedented speed and accuracy. AI powered design assistants can provide valuable insights and recommendations to designers throughout the design process, helping them make more informed decisions and optimize their workflows.

Machine learning algorithms can analyze vast amounts of data and identify patterns and trends that would be impossible for humans to detect, enabling designers to uncover hidden insights and opportunities. These technologies are particularly useful for designers working in data-driven fields such as user experience design, data visualization, and predictive modeling, enabling them to create more meaningful and impactful designs.

These examples illustrate the transformative power of cutting edge technologies in the design process, from virtual reality and augmented reality to generative design and computational design to additive manufacturing and artificial intelligence. Embracing these technologies and harnessing their power, designers can push the boundaries of creativity, efficiency, and innovation, creating designs that are more beautiful, functional, and impactful than ever before. As technology continues to evolve and advance, the possibilities for innovation in design are virtually limitless, paving the way for a future where design is at the forefront of solving some of the world's most pressing challenges.

3.3 Consideration of How Technology Enhances Both Form and Function in Design

The harmonious balance between form and function has always been a central concern in design. Technology has emerged as a powerful tool that not only facilitates the realization of aesthetic visions but also enhances the functionality and performance of designs. This part is based on how technology enhances both form and function in design, showcasing examples where technological advancements have led to the creation of designs that are not only visually stunning but also highly functional and efficient.

(a) Integration of Form and Function
Historically, design has often been dichotomized into form versus function, with some arguing that aesthetics should take precedence over utility, while others prioritize functionality over beauty. However, advancements in technology have blurred these distinctions, enabling designers to seamlessly integrate form and function into their creations.

Through the use of digital tools such as parametric modeling, designers can create designs that are both aesthetically pleasing and highly functional. Parametric design allows designers to optimize designs based on specific criteria such as structural integrity, material efficiency, and ergonomic comfort, resulting in designs that are not only visually striking but also highly efficient and ergonomic.

(b) Responsive and Adaptive Design
Technology has enabled the development of responsive and adaptive design solutions that can dynamically adjust to changing conditions and user needs. From responsive facades that adapt to changing weather conditions to adaptive lighting systems that adjust to the preferences of occupants, technology enables designers to create environments that are responsive to the needs and behaviors of users.

For example, smart home devices such as thermostats, lighting systems, and security cameras can be controlled remotely via smartphone apps, allowing users to personalize their environment and optimize energy usage. Similarly, wearable technology such as fitness trackers and smartwatches can provide real time feedback on health and wellness metrics, enabling users to make informed decisions about their lifestyle and behavior.

(c) Sustainable Design and Environmental Performance
Advancements in technology have also enabled designers to create designs that are more sustainable and environmentally friendly. From renewable energy systems to green building materials to zero waste manufacturing processes, technology offers a wide range of tools and techniques for reducing the environmental impact of designs.

For example, parametric design algorithms can optimize designs for energy efficiency, daylighting, and natural ventilation, reducing the need for artificial lighting and HVAC systems. Similarly, digital fabrication technologies such as 3D printing and CNC machining enable designers to minimize material waste and optimize material usage, resulting in more sustainable and eco-friendly designs. Technology has become an indispensable tool for designers seeking to create designs that are both visually stunning and highly functional. By seamlessly integrating form and function, technology enables designers to push the boundaries of creativity and innovation, creating designs that are not only beautiful but also efficient, ergonomic, and sustainable.

From responsive and adaptive design solutions to sustainable design practices to the seamless integration of digital tools and technologies, technology enhances every aspect of the design process, enabling designers to create designs that are more responsive to user needs, more efficient in their use of resources, and more impactful in their contribution to society and the environment. As technology continues to evolve and advance, the possibilities for innovation in design are virtually limitless, paving the way for a future where design is at the forefront of solving some of the world's most pressing challenges.

4
Challenging Traditional Design Norms

In the world of design, tradition often serves as a foundation upon which creativity flourishes. However, challenging traditional design norms can lead to groundbreaking innovations and paradigm shifts. This chapter explores how designers challenge traditional design norms, whether through experimentation with materials, techniques, or ideologies, and how these challenges can pave the way for new perspectives, approaches, and possibilities in design.

4.1 Critique of Established Design Conventions and Norms

Design, like any other discipline, is steeped in tradition and guided by established conventions that shape the way we perceive and interact with the world. From the principles of form following function to the constraints imposed by prevailing aesthetic trends, these norms serve as guiding principles for designers across generations. However, upon closer inspection, it becomes evident that these conventions are not immutable truths but rather constructs shaped by historical context, cultural values, and prevailing ideologies. Through critical inquiry and rigorous analysis, this section deconstructs the underlying assumptions and biases embedded within established design norms, challenging readers to question the validity of tradition and envision alternative paradigms that better reflect the complexities of contemporary society.

By interrogating the principles of symmetry, balance, and proportion, we uncover the inherent subjectivity and cultural bias that underlie traditional notions of beauty and harmony. Similarly, by scrutinizing the dichotomy between form and function, we reveal the artificial constraints that limit the creative potential of design and hinder innovation. Through thought provoking discourse and illustrative examples, readers are encouraged to challenge preconceived notions and embrace a more expansive definition of design that transcends traditional boundaries and embraces diversity, inclusivity, and experimentation.

As we navigate the intricacies of tradition and innovation within the field of design, it becomes clear that the path to true creativity lies in the willingness to challenge established norms and forge new territories of expression. By interrogating tradition, we open ourselves up to the possibility of transformation and renewal, embarking on a journey of discovery that leads us toward new horizons of possibility and potential.

4.2 Exploration of Designers Who Push Boundaries and Challenge the Status Quo

In the ever evolving landscape of design, innovation often springs from the minds of visionary individuals who dare to challenge the status quo and push the boundaries of creativity. This chapter embarks on a captivating exploration of designers who defy convention, disrupt the norm, and inspire transformative change within their respective fields. Through illuminating case studies and insightful analysis, readers are invited to embark on a journey of discovery, celebrating the pioneering spirit of those who dare to dream and reimagine the possibilities of design.

(a) Zaha Hadid

A Visionary Architect Redefining Space: Zaha Hadid stands as a towering figure in the world of architecture, renowned for her bold vision, avant-garde designs, and unwavering commitment to pushing the limits of what is possible. With iconic projects such as the Heydar Aliyev Center in Baku and the London Aquatics Centre, Hadid shattered conventional notions of form and structure, introducing a new language of fluidity, dynamism, and innovation to the built environment. Through her fearless experimentation and relentless pursuit of excellence, she challenged the architectural establishment, inspiring a new generation of designers to think outside the box and embrace bold, visionary ideas.

(b) Dieter Rams

A Design Icon Embracing Minimalism and Functionality. Dieter Rams is synonymous with timeless design, his work for Braun and his principles of "good design" have left an indelible mark on the field of industrial design. With a philosophy rooted in simplicity, functionality, and user centricity, Rams challenged the prevailing trends of his time, advocating for a return to essentialism and a rejection of excess and ornamentation. Through iconic products such as the Braun SK4 record player and the 606 shelving system, Rams demonstrated the transformative power of minimalism, inspiring designers to prioritize clarity, efficiency, and elegance in their creations.

(c) Yohji Yamamoto

A Fashion Maverick Redefining Beauty and Identity. Yohji Yamamoto is a trailblazer in the world of fashion, renowned for his avant-garde designs, deconstructivist aesthetic, and subversive approach to gender norms. With collections that challenge traditional notions of beauty, femininity, and masculinity, Yamamoto defies categorization, blurring the lines between art, fashion, and identity. Through his innovative use of asymmetry, draping, and unconventional materials, he creates garments that are as thought provoking as they are visually striking, inviting wearers to embrace individuality, self expression, and the inherent beauty of imperfection.

As we journey through the lives and works of these visionary designers, we are reminded of the transformative power of creativity, courage, and imagination. Challenging traditional norms and pushing the boundaries of what is possible, they inspire us to think differently, take risks, and embrace the unknown. Through their pioneering spirit, they pave the way for a more inclusive, innovative, and vibrant future for design, where diversity, experimentation, and authenticity reign supreme.

4.3 Analysis of the Impact of Breaking Traditional Design Rules on Creativity and Innovation

In the dynamic world of design, the act of breaking traditional rules and conventions often catalyzes creativity, innovation, and progress. This chapter explores deep into the transformative effects of challenging established norms, exploring how daring to defy tradition can spark new ideas, inspire fresh perspectives, and propel the field of design into uncharted territory.

(a) Unleashing Creativity Through Disruption
When designers break free from the constraints of tradition, they open themselves up to a world of boundless creativity and imagination. By challenging established rules and conventions, they invite innovation, experimentation, and risk taking into their creative process, giving rise to unexpected solutions and groundbreaking ideas. Through daring acts of disruption, designers shatter the status quo, paving the way for new possibilities and pushing the boundaries of what is deemed possible. Whether it's experimenting with unconventional materials, reimagining familiar forms, or embracing alternative aesthetics, the act of breaking traditional design rules serves as a powerful catalyst for creative expression and innovation.

(b) Inspiring New Perspectives Through Contrarian Thinking
In challenging traditional design norms, designers often adopt a contrarian mindset, questioning prevailing assumptions and seeking alternative viewpoints. By challenging the dominant paradigm, they invite critical reflection, dialogue, and debate, fostering a culture of intellectual curiosity and open mindedness within the design community. Through their willingness to challenge the status quo, they inspire others to think differently, question authority, and explore new avenues of inquiry. Embracing diversity of thought and embracing dissent, they create space for fresh perspectives to emerge, driving innovation and pushing the field of design forward.

(c) Propelling Progress Through Paradigm Shifts
The act of breaking traditional design rules has the power to catalyze paradigm shifts, transforming the way we perceive, interact with, and inhabit the world around us. By challenging entrenched norms and conventions, designers disrupt existing power structures, dismantle outdated systems, and pave the way for new modes of thinking and being. Through their bold acts of defiance, they ignite movements, spark revolutions, and usher in new eras of creativity and innovation. Whether

it's reimagining the relationship between form and function, challenging the boundaries of aesthetics, or advocating for more inclusive and equitable design practices, designers who dare to break tradition have the potential to reshape the very fabric of society and propel us towards a more vibrant, sustainable, and just future.

As we reflect on the transformative impact of breaking traditional design rules, we are reminded of the boundless potential of human creativity and imagination. Daring to challenge the status quo, designers unleash a wave of innovation and inspiration that reverberates across disciplines, pushing the boundaries of what is deemed possible and opening up new frontiers of exploration and discovery. Through their courageous acts of defiance, they remind us that true progress lies in embracing uncertainty, embracing diversity, and daring to imagine a world that has yet to be realized.

5

Shaping the Future of Design Industry

In the labyrinth of creativity, where innovation intertwines with imagination, lies the future of the design industry, waiting to be sculpted by the hands of visionaries and dreamers. This chapter embarks on a journey through the ever evolving landscape of design, exploring the myriad ways in which the industry is shaping the future, molding it into a tapestry of possibility and promise.

5.1 Forecasting Future Trends and Directions in The Design Industry

As the sun sets on the horizon of yesterday, the dawn of a new era of design emerges, painted with bold strokes of creativity and ingenuity. The future of the design industry is a canvas waiting to be filled with the colors of innovation, experimentation, and collaboration.

In this brave new world, designers are not mere creators of objects but architects of experiences, shaping the way we interact with the world around us. From augmented reality to artificial intelligence to sustainable design, the future of the design industry is defined by a relentless pursuit of possibility, pushing the boundaries of what is possible and redefining the very essence of design itself.

(a) The Rise of Sustainable Design
One of the most prominent trends shaping the future of the design industry is the rise of sustainable design. As awareness of environmental issues

grows and consumers become more eco-conscious, there is a growing demand for designs that prioritize sustainability and minimize environmental impact. From eco-friendly materials to energy efficient technologies to circular design principles, sustainable design is reshaping the way designers approach their craft. In the future, we can expect to see an increased emphasis on sustainability across all sectors of the design industry, from architecture and interior design to product design and fashion.

(b) The Convergence of Physical and Digital Desig
Another key trend shaping the future of the design industry is the convergence of physical and digital design. As technology continues to advance and become increasingly integrated into our daily lives, designers are exploring new ways to blend the physical and digital worlds to create immersive and interactive experiences. Augmented reality (AR), virtual reality (VR), and mixed reality (MR) technologies are becoming increasingly prevalent in the design process, allowing designers to create digital prototypes, visualize designs in real world contexts, and engage with users in new and exciting ways. In the future, we can expect to see even greater integration of digital technologies into the design process, blurring the lines between the physical and digital realms.

(c) The Rise of Inclusive Design
Inclusivity is emerging as a central theme in the future of the design industry, with designers increasingly focused on creating designs that are accessible and inclusive for people of all abilities, ages, and backgrounds. Inclusive design goes beyond compliance with accessibility standards to create designs that are inherently welcoming and accommodating to diverse users. From universal design principles to accessible interfaces to inclusive spaces, designers are reimagining the way we approach design to ensure that everyone has equal access to products, services, and experiences. In the future, we can expect to see a greater emphasis on inclusive design across all sectors of the design industry, as designers strive to create a more equitable and inclusive world for all.

(d) The Empowerment of Co-Creation
Collaboration and co-creation are becoming increasingly important in the future of the design industry, as designers recognize the value of working

together with clients, users, and stakeholders to create meaningful and impactful designs. Co-creation empowers users to become active participants in the design process, fostering a sense of ownership and investment in the outcome.

From participatory design workshops to crowdsourced design competitions to open source design platforms, co-creation is reshaping the way designers approach their work, democratizing the design process and ensuring that diverse perspectives are heard and valued. In the future, we can expect to see even greater emphasis on co-creation and collaboration in the design industry, as designers harness the collective wisdom and creativity of the crowd to solve complex challenges and create designs that truly resonate with users.

5.2 Discussion on the Role of Design in Shaping Society and Culture

Design is not just about creating beautiful objects; it's about shaping the way we live, work, and interact with the world around us. From the buildings we inhabit to the products we use to the experiences we enjoy, design plays a central role in shaping society and culture in profound and meaningful ways.

(a) Design as a Reflection of Cultural Identity

One of the most important roles of design is its ability to reflect and celebrate cultural identity. Whether through architecture, fashion, or graphic design, designers have the power to capture the essence of a culture and express it in tangible and visible forms. For example, traditional architecture reflects the values, beliefs, and traditions of a society, while fashion serves as a form of self expression and identity. By embracing cultural diversity and celebrating different cultural traditions, designers can create designs that resonate with people on a deep and personal level, fostering a sense of connection and belonging.

(b) Design as a Catalyst for Social Change

Design has the power to spark social change and challenge the status quo, addressing pressing issues such as inequality, injustice, and environmental degradation. Whether through advocacy campaigns, community led initiatives, or design activism, designers can use their skills and talents to make a positive impact on society. For example, designers may create products that address social and environmental issues, such as sustainable fashion or affordable housing. They may also use design to raise awareness of important social issues and advocate for change, such as through graphic design campaigns or public art installations.

(c) Design as a Driver of Economic Growth
Design is also a powerful driver of economic growth and prosperity, driving innovation, entrepreneurship, and job creation. From startups and small businesses to large corporations and multinational companies, design plays a central role in driving economic development and competitiveness in the global marketplace. For example, design led companies are often more innovative and agile, able to respond quickly to changing market demands and customer needs. By investing in design and fostering a culture of creativity and innovation, countries can stimulate economic growth, create jobs, and enhance their competitiveness on the world stage.

(d) Design as a Source of Inspiration and Joy
Ultimately, design has the power to inspire and uplift us, bringing beauty, joy, and meaning into our lives. Whether through art, architecture, or everyday objects, design to evoke emotions, stimulate the senses, and create memorable experiences. For example, a beautifully designed building can uplift a community and instill a sense of pride and belonging, while a well designed product can enhance our daily lives and bring us joy. By embracing the transformative power of design, we can create a more vibrant, inclusive, and harmonious world for all.

5.3 Consideration of Emerging Technologies and Their Potential Impact on Design Practices

As technology continues to advance at an exponential rate, designers are faced with a dizzying array of new tools, materials, and techniques to explore and experiment with. From artificial intelligence to robotics to 3D printing, emerging technologies have the potential to revolutionize the way designers approach their craft and create new possibilities for innovation and creativity.

(a) Artificial Intelligence and Machine Learning

Artificial intelligence (AI) and machine learning are poised to revolutionize the design industry, enabling designers to automate repetitive tasks, generate creative ideas, and analyze complex datasets with unprecedented speed and accuracy. AI powered design assistants can provide valuable insights and recommendations to designers throughout the design process, helping them make more informed decisions and optimize their workflows. For example, machine learning algorithms can analyze vast amounts of data and identify patterns and trends that would be impossible for humans to detect, enabling designers to uncover hidden insights and opportunities. These technologies are particularly useful for designers working in data driven fields such as user experience design, data visualization, and predictive modeling, enabling them to create more meaningful and impactful designs.

(b) Virtual Reality and Augmented Reality

Virtual reality (VR) and augmented reality (AR) are revolutionizing the way designers visualize and interact with their designs, providing immersive and interactive experiences that engage users in new and exciting ways. VR allows designers to immerse themselves in virtual environments and explore their designs from every angle, providing valuable insights into spatial relationships, scale, and proportion. For example, architects can use VR to create immersive walkthroughs of their designs, allowing clients and stakeholders to experience the space before it is built. Similarly, product designers can use AR to overlay digital information onto the physical world, enabling users to interact with virtual models in real world environments.

(c) Generative Design and Computational Design

Generative design and computational design are computational approaches to design that use algorithms to generate and optimize form and structure based on predefined criteria and constraints. These technologies enable designers to explore a vast range of design options and identify the most optimal solutions based on performance, efficiency, and aesthetics. For example, generative design algorithms can optimize designs for specific criteria such as weight, material usage, and structural integrity, resulting in highly efficient and optimized designs. Similarly, computational design algorithms can create complex geometries and patterns that respond to specific parameters and constraints, enabling designers to create intricate and organic forms that would be impossible to achieve using traditional design methods.

(d) Additive Manufacturing (3D Printing)

Additive manufacturing, also known as 3D printing, is revolutionizing the way designers create and fabricate objects, enabling them to produce complex and customized designs with unprecedented precision and efficiency. Unlike traditional manufacturing methods, which involve subtracting material from a solid block, additive manufacturing builds objects layer by layer from digital models, allowing for greater design freedom and flexibility. For example, designers can use 3D printing to create prototypes, custom components, and finished products with intricate geometries that would be impossible to achieve using traditional manufacturing methods. These technologies are particularly useful for designers working in fields such as product design, architecture, and fashion, enabling them to create designs that are more innovative, efficient, and sustainable.

The future of the design industry is a tapestry of trends and directions, woven together by the threads of creativity, innovation, and sustainability. From the rise of sustainable design to the convergence of physical and digital design to the empowerment of co-creation, the future of the design industry is defined by a relentless pursuit of possibility and promise. By embracing diversity, fostering collaboration, and harnessing the transformative power of emerging technologies, designers can shape the future of the design industry into a masterpiece of creativity, innovation, and impact, paving the way for a brighter and more beautiful world for all.

6

Embracing Creativity and Experimentation

Creativity and experimentation are essential for pushing design forward and producing innovative solutions. Designers must foster an environment that encourages thinking outside the box and taking risks to uncover new possibilities.

In the exhilarating world of design, where imagination knows no bounds and innovation reigns supreme, the ethos of embracing creativity and experimentation serves as the cornerstone of progress and transformation. This chapter explores into the profound significance of fostering an environment that nurtures creativity and encourages risk taking, celebrating the fearless innovators who dare to push the boundaries of conventional design and pave the way for groundbreaking discoveries and visionary solutions.

6.1 Advocacy For Fostering Creativity and Experimentation in Design

Advocacy for creativity and experimentation starts by recognizing their value. Unconventional and original thinking enables designers to uncover unique solutions that conventional wisdom might overlook. Experimentation helps in testing new ideas that could yield unexpected benefits. Organizations should reward, not punish, attempts at creativity that do not pan out, as learning from failures often informs future successes. Designers must make a case for the strategic importance of creativity and experimentation to gain support from leadership.

Creativity is the lifeblood of the design industry, fueling the ingenuity and vision that propel it forward into uncharted territories of possibility. By fostering a culture of innovation, organizations can unlock new opportunities, discover untapped markets, and differentiate themselves from competitors. Moreover, creativity and experimentation are paramount for attracting and retaining top talent in the design industry. In a world where creativity is highly prized, companies that foster a culture of innovation are more likely to attract ambitious and talented designers who are passionate about pushing the boundaries of what is possible.

Believers of creativity and experimentation in design passionately argue that these qualities are not only desirable but essential for unlocking new possibilities, addressing complex challenges, and shaping the future of the industry. Here, we explore the compelling case for embracing creativity and experimentation in design:

(a) Fueling Innovation and Breakthroughs
Creativity is the lifeblood of the design industry, propelling it forward and inspiring breakthroughs that push the boundaries of what is possible. By fostering a culture of creativity and experimentation, organizations can unlock new opportunities, discover untapped markets, and differentiate themselves from competitors.

(b) Driving Growth and Adaptability
In an increasingly complex and competitive global marketplace, organizations that embrace creativity and experimentation are better equipped to adapt to changing trends, evolving customer preferences, and emerging technologies. Designers who are encouraged to explore new ideas, take risks, and experiment with different approaches are more likely to produce innovative solutions that meet the needs of a rapidly changing world.

(c) Inspiring Collaboration and Diversity
Creativity thrives in environments where diverse perspectives, experiences, and ideas are valued and celebrated. By fostering a culture of creativity and experimentation, organizations can inspire collaboration,

foster inclusivity, and harness the collective intelligence of their teams. Designers from diverse backgrounds bring unique insights and approaches to the table, leading to richer, more innovative solutions that resonate with a broader audience.

(d) Cultivating a Growth Mindset

Embracing creativity and experimentation requires a shift in mindset from a fixed to a growth oriented perspective. Designers who are encouraged to experiment, take risks, and learn from failure develop a growth mindset that enables them to adapt, evolve, and thrive in an ever changing environment. Cultivating a culture of continuous learning and improvement empowers organizations to help their teams embrace challenges, overcome obstacles, and achieve greater levels of creativity and innovation.

(e) Creating Meaningful and Memorable Experiences

Design has the power to shape human experiences, evoke emotions, and create lasting impressions. By embracing creativity and experimentation, designers can create meaningful and memorable experiences that engage, inspire, and delight users. Whether it's through innovative products, immersive environments, or compelling storytelling, creativity and experimentation are essential for creating designs that resonate on a deep and personal level.

(f) Fostering a Sense of Purpose and Fulfillment

Creativity and experimentation are not only essential for driving business success but also for fostering a sense of purpose and fulfillment among designers. Designers who are given the freedom to explore their passions, pursue their interests, and express their creativity are more likely to feel fulfilled and engaged in their work. By prioritizing creativity and experimentation, organizations can create a work environment where designers feel empowered to unleash their full creative potential and make a meaningful impact on the world around them.

The support for fostering creativity and experimentation in design is rooted in the belief that these qualities are fundamental to driving innovation, inspiring collaboration, and creating meaningful experiences. Embracing creativity and experimentation enables organizations to unlock new opportunities, drive growth, and shape the future of the industry in profound and transformative ways. As we champion creativity and experimentation in design, we pave the way for a future filled with innovation, inspiration, and endless possibilities.

6.2 Strategies For Encouraging Risk Taking and Innovation in Design Processes

Encouraging risk taking and fostering innovation is crucial for pushing the boundaries of design and driving progress in the industry. Design processes that embrace experimentation and creativity are more likely to yield breakthrough solutions and transformative outcomes. Here, we explore several strategies for cultivating an environment that encourages risk taking and innovation in design processes:

(a) Create a Culture of Psychological Safety

Design teams thrive in environments where they feel safe to take risks and share their ideas without fear of judgment or reprisal. Leaders should foster a culture of psychological safety by encouraging open communication, embracing failure as a learning opportunity, and celebrating experimentation.

(b) Provide Time and Resources for Exploration

Allocate dedicated time and resources for designers to explore new ideas, experiment with different approaches, and pursue passion projects. Designers who have the freedom to explore and innovate without the pressure of immediate deadlines are more likely to produce novel and inventive solutions.

(c) Encourage Interdisciplinary Collaboration:

Foster collaboration between designers, engineers, marketers, and other stakeholders to bring diverse perspectives and expertise to the design process. Interdisciplinary collaboration encourages cross-pollination of ideas and fosters a culture of innovation by challenging assumptions and sparking new insights.

(d) Embrace Design Thinking Methodologies

Adopt design thinking methodologies, such as empathy driven design and rapid prototyping, to encourage iterative experimentation and user centered innovation. Design thinking empowers teams to empathize with end users, define problems creatively, generate multiple solutions, and test ideas quickly to identify the most promising concepts.

(e) Celebrate Risk taking and Failure

Recognize and celebrate designers who take risks and push the boundaries of what is possible. Highlighting success stories and lessons learned from failure helps to destigmatize risk taking and encourages others to embrace experimentation and innovation.

(f) Provide Access to Cutting edge Tools and Technologies

Invest in state of the art tools, technologies, and resources that empower designers to push the limits of their creativity. Whether it's access to advanced software, prototyping equipment, or materials, providing designers with the right tools can catalyze innovation and enable them to bring their ideas to life.

(g) Encourage Cross-functional Learning and Skill Development

Foster a culture of continuous learning and skill development by providing opportunities for designers to expand their knowledge and expertise beyond their core discipline. Encouraging designers to learn new skills, explore different domains, and collaborate with experts from other fields can inspire fresh perspectives and innovative approaches to problem solving.

(h) Promote Autonomy and Ownership

Empower designers to take ownership of their projects and make autonomous decisions about design direction and execution. Giving designers the freedom to pursue their ideas and take calculated risks fosters a sense of ownership and accountability, leading to more innovative and impactful outcomes.

(i) Provide Mentorship and Support

Pair less experienced designers with mentors who can provide guidance, support, and encouragement as they navigate the challenges of the design process. Mentorship programs help to cultivate a culture of learning, growth, and risk taking by providing designers with the resources and support they need to succeed.

(j) Lead by Example

Leadership plays a crucial role in fostering a culture of innovation and risk taking. Leaders should lead by example by demonstrating a willingness to take risks, embrace uncertainty, and champion experimentation. When leaders prioritize innovation and encourage their teams to push the boundaries of what is possible, it sets the tone for a culture that values creativity, curiosity, and courage.

By implementing these strategies, organizations can create an environment that empowers designers to take risks, experiment with new ideas, and push the boundaries of innovation in the design process. Encouraging risk taking and fostering a culture of innovation not only drives progress and propels the industry forward but also inspires teams to reach new heights of creativity and excellence.

6.3 Examples Of Designers Who Embrace Unconventional Approaches to Their Work

In the dynamic world of design, there are visionary creators who defy convention, challenge norms, and push the boundaries of what is possible. These designers are fearless innovators, unafraid to experiment, explore, and reimagine the possibilities of their craft. Here, we explore the stories of some of these remarkable individuals whose unconventional approaches have left an indelible mark on the design landscape.

(a) Stefan Sagmeister

Stefan Sagmeister, an Austrian born graphic designer, is renowned for his daring and provocative approach to design. His work is characterized by its bold experimentation with typography, imagery, and materials, challenging viewers to reconsider their perceptions of graphic design. Sagmeister's unconventional designs often incorporate unexpected elements, such as handcrafted typography made from unconventional materials like bananas or even his own body. His willingness to push the boundaries of traditional graphic design has earned him widespread acclaim and recognition as one of the most influential designers of his generation.

(b) Neri Oxman
Neri Oxman is a pioneering architect, designer, and professor known for her groundbreaking work in the fields of computational design and digital fabrication. Inspired by nature and biology, Oxman's designs blur the boundaries between art, architecture, and science, pushing the limits of what is possible with advanced technologies such as 3D printing and robotics. Her work often explores themes of biomimicry, sustainability, and the integration of technology and nature, resulting in designs that are both innovative and environmentally conscious. Oxman's unconventional approach to design has garnered international acclaim and cemented her reputation as a leading figure in the field of experimental architecture and design.

(c) Yves Béhar
Yves Béhar is a Swiss born industrial designer known for his humancentered approach to design and his commitment to creating products that enhance the human experience. Béhar's designs often feature sleek and minimalist aesthetics, combined with innovative technologies and sustainable materials. His work spans a wide range of industries, from furniture and consumer electronics to transportation and wearable technology. Béhar is particularly known for his collaborations with companies such as Jawbone, Herman Miller, and Airbnb, where he has brought his unique blend of creativity, innovation, and social responsibility to bear on some of the most pressing challenges of our time.

(d) Karim Rashid
Karim Rashid is an Egyptian born industrial designer known for his colorful and playful aesthetic and his prolific output across a wide range of design disciplines. Rashid's designs often feature bold colors, organic shapes, and innovative materials, reflecting his belief that good design should be accessible, affordable, and inclusive. His work encompasses everything from furniture and lighting to fashion and packaging, with collaborations with companies such as Alessi, Umbra, and Samsung. Rashid's unconventional approach to design has earned him numerous awards and accolades and has cemented his reputation as one of the most influential designers of his generation.

(e) Zaha Hadid

Zaha Hadid was a trailblazing architect known for her avant-garde designs and groundbreaking approach to architecture. Throughout her career, Hadid challenged the conventions of traditional architecture, pushing the boundaries of form, space, and materiality. Her designs often feature sweeping curves, dynamic geometries, and innovative structural systems, creating buildings that are as visually striking as they are structurally innovative. Hadid's exceptional approach to architecture has earned her numerous awards and accolades, including the Pritzker Architecture Prize, and has cemented her legacy as one of the most influential architects of the 21st century.

These designers exemplify the spirit of innovation and experimentation that defines the world of design. Through their fearless exploration of new ideas, materials, and technologies, they have expanded the possibilities of what design can achieve and inspired countless others to follow in their footsteps. As we celebrate their contributions to the field of design, we are reminded of the transformative power of creativity, curiosity, and courage in shaping the world around us.

7

Redefining the Boundaries of Design

In the dynamic and ever evolving landscape of design, the boundaries between disciplines are becoming increasingly blurred, giving rise to new opportunities for innovation and creativity. This chapter explores interdisciplinary approaches to design, where collaboration, integration, and cross-pollination of ideas redefine what it means to design in the 21st century.

7.1 Exploration of Interdisciplinary Approaches to Design

Traditionally, design has been viewed through a narrow lens, confined to specific disciplines such as graphic design, industrial design, or architecture. However, the boundaries of design are no longer rigidly defined, but rather fluid and permeable, allowing for the convergence of diverse disciplines and methodologies.

Interdisciplinary approaches to design embrace the idea that complex problems cannot be solved within the confines of a single discipline but require integrating knowledge, expertise, and perspectives from multiple fields. By bringing together designers, engineers, scientists, artists, and other experts from diverse backgrounds, interdisciplinary design seeks to tackle complex challenges from multiple angles and create holistic solutions that address the needs of a rapidly changing world.

One example of interdisciplinary design is the field of "biomimicry," which draws inspiration from nature to solve human problems. By studying the principles and patterns found in the natural world, designers can create innovative solutions that are not only more sustainable but also more efficient and resilient. From architecture inspired by termite mounds to materials inspired by spider silk, biomimicry demonstrates the power of interdisciplinary collaboration in design.

Another example is the field of "design thinking," which applies the principles and methodologies of design to solve complex problems in business, education, healthcare, and beyond. By adopting a human centered approach to problem solving, design thinking empowers teams to empathize with end users, define problems creatively, generate multiple solutions, and test ideas iteratively. Design thinking transcends traditional disciplinary boundaries, emphasizing collaboration, creativity, and empathy as essential components of the design process.

Furthermore, the rise of "inclusive design" underscores the importance of considering the diverse needs and perspectives of users in the design process. By incorporating principles of accessibility, diversity, and equity, inclusive design seeks to create products, services, and environments that are usable and meaningful for people of all abilities, ages, and backgrounds. Inclusive design challenges designers to think beyond their own experiences and biases, fostering empathy, understanding, and social responsibility in the design process.

The exploration of interdisciplinary approaches to design represents a paradigm shift in the way we conceive of and practice design. By embracing collaboration, integration, and cross-pollination of ideas, interdisciplinary design expands the boundaries of what is possible and creates new opportunities for innovation and creativity. As we continue to redefine the boundaries of design, we pave the way for a future that is more inclusive, sustainable, and human centric

7.2 Intersections of Design with Psychology, Sociology, and Anthropology

The convergence of design with disciplines like psychology, sociology, and anthropology opens up a vast realm of possibilities, enriching the practice of design with insights into human behavior, cultural dynamics, and societal needs. This discussion explores how design intersects with these fields and the profound impact it has on shaping human experiences, behaviors, and societies.

Psychology: Understanding Human Behavior and Emotion

Design and psychology share a common focus on understanding human behavior, cognition, and emotion, making them natural allies in the pursuit of creating designs that resonate with users on a deep and emotional level. Designers draw upon principles of psychology to inform decisions about user interface design, color psychology, user experience (UX) design, and behavioral economics.

For example, in the area of UX design, designers leverage cognitive psychology insights to create intuitive, user friendly interfaces and conducive to positive user experiences. By understanding how users perceive, process, and interact with digital interfaces, designers can optimize the design of websites, applications, and digital products to meet the needs and preferences of their target audience.

In addition, psychology plays a crucial role in the design of products and environments that evoke specific emotions and responses in users. Designers use principles of emotional design to create products that inspire joy, surprise, delight, or even nostalgia, tapping into the psychological aspects of human perception and experience to create memorable and impactful designs.

Sociology: Designing for Communities and Societal Impact

Design and sociology intersect in social design, where designers collaborate with communities and stakeholders to address social issues, foster inclusivity, and promote positive societal change. Social designers draw upon principles of sociology to understand the needs, values, and dynamics of communities and to design solutions that address systemic inequalities, promote social cohesion, and empower marginalized groups.

For example, in urban design, designers work closely with sociologists to create inclusive and equitable public spaces that meet the diverse needs of urban populations. By engaging with communities through participatory design processes, designers can ensure that their designs reflect the lived experiences and aspirations of the people who use them, fostering a sense of ownership and belonging among residents.

In addition, design interventions in areas such as healthcare, education, and sustainability often draw upon sociological principles to address complex social problems and promote positive societal outcomes. By collaborating with sociologists and other social scientists, designers can develop solutions that are grounded in evidence based research, culturally sensitive, and contextually relevant, leading to more effective and sustainable interventions.

Anthropology: Designing for Cultural Understanding and Context
Design and anthropology converge in the realm of cultural design, where designers draw upon insights from anthropology to create products, services, and environments that are culturally sensitive, contextually appropriate, and respectful of diverse cultural traditions and practices. Anthropological perspectives inform the design process by providing insights into the cultural meanings, values, and rituals that shape human behavior and interactions.

For example, in the design of global brands and products, designers work with anthropologists to conduct cultural research and ethnographic studies to understand the cultural nuances and preferences of different target markets. By incorporating cultural insights into the design process, designers can create products that resonate with local audiences, avoid cultural misunderstandings, and build trust and authenticity with consumers.

In addition, anthropology plays a crucial role in the design of products and services for indigenous communities and marginalized populations. By collaborating with anthropologists and community members, designers can co-create solutions that are culturally appropriate, socially inclusive, and sustainable, respecting the traditions, knowledge, and rights of the people they serve.

(a) Psychology and Design for Understanding Human Behavior and Emotion
The intersection of psychology and design delves into the intricate relationship between human cognition, emotion, and behavior, shaping the

way we perceive, interact with, and respond to design. By drawing upon principles of cognitive psychology, designers can create experiences that resonate with users on a subconscious level, evoking emotions, influencing decision making, and fostering engagement.

For instance, the use of color, typography, and imagery in graphic design can evoke specific emotions and associations, influencing how users perceive and interpret visual messages. Similarly, in user experience (UX) design, principles of cognitive psychology inform the design of interfaces that are intuitive, user friendly, and conducive to positive user experiences.

Moreover, insights from social psychology illuminate the role of social norms, group dynamics, and identity in shaping behavior and preferences, informing design strategies for creating inclusive, community oriented spaces and products. By understanding the psychological drivers behind user behavior, designers can create solutions that resonate with users on a deeper, more meaningful level.

(b) Sociology and Design for Communities and Societal Impact

The intersection of sociology and design explores the complex interplay between individuals, communities, and broader societal structures, informing design solutions that address social needs, promote equity, and foster social cohesion. By drawing upon sociological theories and methodologies, designers can develop solutions that are responsive to the diverse needs, values, and aspirations of different social groups.

Such as in urban design and planning, sociological insights into patterns of social interaction, mobility, and access to resources inform the design of inclusive, equitable cities that prioritize the well being and participation of all residents. Similarly, in product design, sociological research helps designers understand the cultural, economic, and social factors that shape user preferences and behaviors, informing the design of products that are culturally sensitive, accessible, and relevant to diverse populations.

(c) Anthropology and Design for Cultural Understanding and Context

The intersection of anthropology and design explores the rich tapestry of human cultures, traditions, and practices, informing design solutions that are deeply rooted in the lived experiences and cultural contexts of users. By drawing upon ethnographic research methods and anthropological theories, designers can gain insights into the values, beliefs, and rituals that shape human behavior and inform the design of culturally resonant solutions.

Such as, in service design, anthropological insights into user behaviors, rituals, and social norms inform the design of services that are tailored to the needs and preferences of specific cultural groups. Similarly, in product design, anthropological research helps designers understand the cultural meanings and symbolic associations attached to products, informing the design of products that reflect and celebrate diverse cultural identities.

The intersections of design with psychology, sociology, and anthropology enrich the practice of design with deep insights into human behavior, social dynamics, and cultural contexts. By drawing upon principles and methodologies from these fields, designers can develop solutions that are not only aesthetically pleasing and functional but also empathetic, inclusive, and responsive to the diverse needs and aspirations of users. As we continue to explore the synergies between design and these disciplines, we pave the way for a future where design plays a central role in addressing complex societal challenges and shaping a more equitable, sustainable, and inclusive world.

7.3 Case Studies Demonstrating the Power of Inter-disciplinary Collaboration in Design Projects

Interdisciplinary collaboration in design projects brings together diverse perspectives, expertise, and methodologies to tackle complex challenges and create innovative solutions that transcend traditional boundaries. The following case studies illustrate how interdisciplinary teams leverage insights from psychology, sociology, anthropology, and other fields to address real world problems and create impactful design solutions:

(a) The Dementia Village, Hogeweyk (Netherlands)

The Dementia Village, located in Hogeweyk, Netherlands, is a pioneering example of interdisciplinary collaboration in healthcare design. Conceived as a residential care facility for elderly residents with dementia, the village is designed to mimic a small, self contained community, complete with streets, shops, and communal spaces. Interdisciplinary teams of architects, healthcare professionals, psychologists, and social workers collaborated to design a living environment that supports the unique needs and preferences of residents with dementia, promoting autonomy, independence, and quality of life. The village's design incorporates principles of wayfinding, sensory stimulation, and familiar environments to create a safe and nurturing environment for residents, enabling them to maintain a sense of dignity and purpose amidst their cognitive challenges.

(b) MIT Media Lab's City Science Initiative (United States)
The MIT Media Lab's City Science Initiative is a multidisciplinary research project that brings together experts from fields such as urban planning, architecture, computer science, and transportation engineering to explore innovative solutions for urban mobility and sustainability. Through interdisciplinary collaboration, researchers develop cutting edge technologies, such as autonomous vehicles, smart infrastructure, and data driven urban planning tools, to address pressing urban challenges and shape the cities of the future. By integrating insights from diverse disciplines, the City Science Initiative aims to create more livable, equitable, and sustainable urban environments that enhance the quality of life for residents and promote economic prosperity.

(c) Nike Flyknit Innovation (Global)
Nike's Flyknit technology is a testament to the power of interdisciplinary collaboration in product design and innovation. By bringing together designers, engineers, materials scientists, and athletes, Nike developed Flyknit, a revolutionary manufacturing process that uses computer controlled knitting machines to create seamless, lightweight, and customizable footwear. Interdisciplinary teams collaborated to optimize the design and performance of Flyknit shoes, balancing factors such as durability, breathability, and comfort to meet the diverse needs of athletes across different sports and disciplines. The result is a range of innovative footwear products that push the boundaries of performance, comfort, and sustainability, revolutionizing the athletic footwear industry and setting new standards for design and innovation.

(d) The High Line, New York City (United States)
The High Line, a linear park built on a historic elevated railway viaduct in New York City, is a prime example of interdisciplinary collaboration in urban design and revitalization. Architects, landscape architects, urban

planners, artists, and community stakeholders came together to transform a disused industrial infrastructure into a vibrant public space that celebrates the city's history, culture, and community. Through interdisciplinary collaboration, the project integrated ecological design principles, public art installations, and community engagement initiatives to create a unique urban oasis that reconnects residents and visitors with nature, history, and each other. The High Line has become a model for sustainable urban development and placemaking, inspiring similar projects around the world.

The High Line, an elevated linear park built on a historic freight rail line in Manhattan, serves as a compelling example of interdisciplinary collaboration in urban design. Landscape architects, architects, urban planners, and community stakeholders collaborated to transform an abandoned railway into a vibrant public space that celebrates nature, history, and community.

Psychological principles informed the design of the park's layout, amenities, and programming to enhance user experience and well being. Sociological research guided efforts to create inclusive spaces that cater to the diverse needs and preferences of local residents, visitors, and communities. Anthropological insights into the cultural significance of the site and its surrounding neighborhoods informed design decisions that honor the area's history, heritage, and sense of place.

(e) IDEO's Patient Experience Design for UCSF Medical Center
IDEO, a global design and innovation consultancy, collaborated with the University of California, San Francisco (UCSF) Medical Center to redesign the patient experience in healthcare settings. Interdisciplinary teams of designers, healthcare professionals, psychologists, and anthropologists worked together to identify pain points, challenges, and opportunities for improvement in the patient journey.

Psychological insights into patient behavior, emotions, and motivations informed the design of physical spaces, digital interfaces, and communication strategies to enhance patient satisfaction and engagement. Sociological research guided efforts to create patient-centered care environments that prioritize dignity, respect, and inclusivity. Anthropological perspectives on cultural diversity and healthcare practices informed design solutions that are sensitive to the needs and preferences of diverse patient populations.

Through interdisciplinary collaboration, IDEO and UCSF Medical Center developed innovative healthcare solutions that prioritize empathy, compassion, and humancentered design, improving the patient experience and transforming the delivery of healthcare services.

(f) Copenhagen's Bicycle-Friendly Infrastructure

Copenhagen, Denmark, is renowned for its bicycle-friendly urban infrastructure, which has been developed through interdisciplinary collaboration between urban planners, transportation engineers, environmental scientists, and community activists. By prioritizing sustainable transportation modes such as cycling, Copenhagen has transformed its urban landscape, reducing traffic congestion, air pollution, and carbon emissions while promoting health, equity, and quality of life.

Psychological principles informed the design of bicycle infrastructure and traffic calming measures to enhance cyclist safety and comfort, encouraging more people to choose cycling as a mode of transportation. Sociological research guided efforts to create inclusive cycling environments that cater to cyclists of all ages, abilities, and backgrounds, fostering a sense of community and belonging.

Through interdisciplinary collaboration, Copenhagen has emerged as a global leader in sustainable urban transportation, demonstrating the power of design to create cities that are healthier, greener, and more livable for all.

In a nutshell, these case studies illustrate the transformative power of interdisciplinary collaboration in design projects, demonstrating how teams of experts from diverse disciplines can come together to tackle complex challenges, drive innovation, and create meaningful impact. By embracing interdisciplinary collaboration, designers can leverage the collective wisdom and expertise of multiple disciplines to develop holistic, integrated solutions that address the multifaceted needs of users and communities, shaping a more equitable, sustainable, and inclusive future for all.

8

Pushing the limits of Imagination

At the forefront of the design world stand visionary designers who defy conventional wisdom, challenge existing paradigms, and push the boundaries of what is possible.

In the realm of design, the future is not merely a destination but a canvas upon which visionary designers paint bold and imaginative visions of what could be. This chapter examines the work of these pioneering individuals, exploring how their relentless pursuit of innovation and imagination has reshaped the landscape of design and inspired generations to dream bigger and bolder.

8.1 Examination of Visionary Designers Who Push the Limits of Imagination

(a) Philippe Starck

Philippe Starck is a French designer known for his bold, avant-garde approach to design across various disciplines, including furniture, interiors, and product design. With a penchant for unconventional forms and materials, Starck's designs challenge traditional notions of aesthetics and functionality, pushing the boundaries of imagination. His iconic creations, such as the Louis Ghost chair and the Juicy Salif citrus juicer, exemplify his commitment to innovation and his ability to merge artistry with functionality in unexpected ways.

(b) Zaha Hadid

Zaha Hadid was a trailblazing architect known for her groundbreaking designs that redefined the possibilities of architecture. With her signature fluid forms, organic geometries, and innovative use of materials, Hadid's buildings challenge the limits of imagination and blur the lines between art and architecture. From the swooping curves of the Guangzhou Opera House to the dynamic angles of the Heydar Aliyev Center, Hadid's visionary designs continue to inspire awe and wonder, pushing the boundaries of what is possible in architecture.

(c) Bjarke Ingels

Bjarke Ingels is a Danish architect known for his visionary approach to architecture, which he describes as "pragmatic utopianism." Through his firm, BIG (Bjarke Ingels Group), Ingels has designed a diverse range of projects that defy convention and challenge traditional architectural norms. From the innovative Amager Bakke waste-to-energy plant, which doubles as a ski slope, to the transformative VIA 57 West residential building in New York City, Ingels' designs push the limits of imagination while addressing pressing social, environmental, and urban challenges.

(d) Olafur Eliasson

Olafur Eliasson is a Danish-Icelandic artist known for his immersive installations and environmental interventions that explore the intersection of art, science, and nature. Through his use of light, color, and natural elements, Eliasson creates transformative experiences that challenge viewers' perceptions and provoke contemplation. From his iconic Weather Project installation at Tate Modern to his recent Earth Perspectives series, Eliasson's visionary works invite viewers to reimagine their relationship with the world around them, pushing the boundaries of imagination and expanding the possibilities of art and design.

(e) Neri Oxman

Neri Oxman is a pioneering designer and architect known for her groundbreaking work in the field of computational design and digital fabrication. Through her research at the MIT Media Lab's Mediated Matter group, Oxman explores the intersection of biology, technology, and design, creating innovative structures and materials inspired by nature. From 3D-printed wearables that respond to environmental stimuli to biofabricated/ biomimetics of the building components grown from living organisms, Oxman's visionary designs challenge the limits of imagination and offer glimpses into a future where design is seamlessly integrated with the natural world.

These visionary designers exemplify the power of imagination to transcend boundaries, defy expectations, and inspire transformative change. Through their bold ideas, innovative approaches, and visionary visions, they push the limits of imagination and pave the way for a future where creativity knows no bounds. As we celebrate their contributions to the world of design, we are reminded of the boundless potential of the human imagination to shape a better, more beautiful world for generations to come.

8.2 Exploration of Speculative and Futuristic Design Concepts

This section embarks on a journey into the world of speculative and futuristic design concepts, where creativity knows no bounds, and the boundaries of possibility are constantly being pushed and redefined.

(a) Speculative Design: Pushing the Boundaries of Imagination

Speculative design is a forward thinking approach that explores alternative futures and possibilities through the lens of design. By imagining scenarios, environments, and technologies that may exist in the future, speculative designers provoke critical reflection, challenge assumptions, and inspire dialogue about the social, cultural, and ethical implications of emerging technologies and trends.

One example of speculative design is the work of Dunne & Raby, who create provocative design fictions that explore potential futures shaped by advances in science, technology, and society. Through their projects, such as "Designs for an Overpopulated Planet: Foragers," they invite viewers to consider the consequences of overpopulation and environmental degradation on human behavior, culture, and lifestyle, challenging us to rethink our assumptions about progress and sustainability. Through speculative artifacts such as the "Huggable Atomic Mushroom" and the "Emotionally Intelligent Toilet," Dunne & Raby challenge viewers to consider the broader implications of technological innovation on society and culture.

Another example is the speculative design work of Superflux, a design studio that creates immersive experiences and interactive installations that invite viewers to imagine alternative futures. Through projects such as "Mitigation of Shock," which explores the consequences of climate change on everyday life, and "Uninvited Guests," which imagines a world where ubiquitous surveillance is the norm, Superflux pushes the boundaries of imagination and encourages viewers to think critically about the future they want to create.

(b) *Futuristic Design Concepts: Envisioning Tomorrow's World*

Futuristic design concepts envision a world transformed by cutting edge technologies, innovative materials, and radical ideas. From utopian visions of a harmonious, technologically advanced society to dystopian nightmares of a world ravaged by climate change and social upheaval, futuristic design concepts offer glimpses into possible futures shaped by human ingenuity and imagination. Futuristic design concepts take inspiration from speculative fiction, science fiction, and emerging technologies to envision bold, visionary futures that challenge our assumptions and expand our horizons. From flying cars to space colonies, futuristic design concepts offer glimpses into a world where anything is possible and imagination knows no limits.

One example of a futuristic design concept is the Hyperloop, a high speed transportation system proposed by entrepreneur Elon Musk. Inspired by the concept of pneumatic tubes, the Hyperloop envisions a network of low pressure tubes through which pods can travel at near supersonic speeds, revolutionizing long distance travel and transportation.

Another example is the concept of vertical farming, which proposes the use of vertical structures and hydroponic systems to grow food in urban environments. By maximizing space and reducing the need for land, water, and pesticides, vertical farming offers a sustainable solution to food security and environmental sustainability challenges in an increasingly urbanized world.

Another example of futuristic design concepts is the work of Tesla, a company known for its innovative electric vehicles and renewable energy solutions. Through projects such as the Tesla Roadster, which aims to revolutionize the automotive industry with its electric powertrain and autonomous driving capabilities, Tesla pushes the boundaries of what is possible in transportation and energy technology.

Another such example is the work of Space X, a private aerospace manufacturer and space transportation company founded by Elon Musk. Through projects such as the Starship spacecraft, which aims to enable human colonization of Mars, SpaceX is pushing the boundaries of space exploration and pioneering new frontiers in human spaceflight.

(c) Designing for the Unknown

As designers explore speculative and futuristic concepts, they confront the inherent uncertainty and ambiguity of the future. Designing for the unknown requires a willingness to embrace uncertainty, take risks, and challenge assumptions about what is possible. It also demands a deep understanding of the social, cultural, and ethical implications of emerging technologies and trends, as well as a commitment to designing solutions that are inclusive, equitable, and sustainable. As technology continues to advance and society evolves, the possibilities for speculative and futuristic design are endless. From augmented reality to artificial intelligence, biotechnology to sustainable architecture, designers are exploring new frontiers and pushing the boundaries of imagination in ways that were once unimaginable.

One approach to designing for the unknown is speculative design fiction, which uses storytelling, visualization, and prototyping to imagine and explore possible futures. By creating immersive narratives and tangible artifacts that embody future scenarios, speculative designers invite audiences to engage with complex issues and envision alternative futures that challenge the status quo.

One emerging trend in speculative and futuristic design is the exploration of immersive experiences and virtual worlds that blur the lines between physical and digital reality. Through projects such as virtual reality theme parks, augmented reality art installations, and mixed reality storytelling experiences, designers are creating new forms of entertainment, education, and social interaction that redefine our relationship with technology and the world around us.

Another emerging trend is the integration of bio-design principles into design practice, where living organisms and biological processes are used to create sustainable, regenerative solutions to environmental challenges. From biofabricated materials to living architecture, bio-design offers new possibilities for creating resilient, adaptive systems that mimic the resilience and efficiency of natural ecosystems.

Lastly, the exploration of speculative and futuristic design concepts offers a glimpse into the boundless potential of human imagination to shape the world of tomorrow. By daring to dream, challenge, and innovate, designers push the boundaries of what is possible and inspire us to imagine futures that are bold, beautiful, and brimming with possibilities. As we embark on this journey into the unknown, let us embrace the power of design to shape a future that is not just technologically advanced, but also socially, culturally, and environmentally sustainable for generations to come.

8.3 Consideration of the Ethical Implications of Radical Design Ideas

In the pursuit of innovation and progress, designers often explore radical ideas that challenge the status quo and push the boundaries of what is possible. However, with great creativity comes great responsibility, and it is essential for designers to consider the ethical implications of their radical design ideas. This chapter examines the ethical dimensions of radical design concepts, exploring the potential risks, benefits, and dilemmas that arise when pushing the limits of imagination.

Balancing Innovation with Responsibility

Radical design ideas have the potential to drive positive change, disrupt industries, and improve quality of life for individuals and communities. However, they also pose ethical dilemmas and risks that must be carefully considered and addressed. Designers must strike a delicate balance between innovation and responsibility, ensuring that their ideas and solutions uphold ethical principles and contribute to the greater good.

(a) Ethical Considerations in Radical Design
   i. **Social Equity and Justice:** Radical design ideas have the power to either exacerbate or mitigate social inequalities and injustices. Designers must consider the potential impact of their ideas on

marginalized communities, vulnerable populations, and future generations. They must strive to create solutions that promote social equity, inclusivity, and justice while avoiding unintended consequences that may perpetuate existing disparities.

ii. **Environmental Sustainability:** Many radical design ideas aim to address pressing environmental challenges, such as climate change, pollution, and resource depletion. While these solutions hold great promise, they may also have unintended environmental consequences, such as habitat destruction, biodiversity loss, and ecosystem disruption. Designers must carefully assess the environmental impacts of their ideas and prioritize sustainability, resilience, and regeneration in their design solutions.

iii. **Privacy and Data Security:** In an increasingly connected and digitized world, radical design ideas often involve the collection, analysis, and utilization of vast amounts of personal data. Designers must consider the ethical implications of data privacy, security, and consent, ensuring that their solutions respect individuals' rights to privacy, autonomy, and control over their personal information.

iv. **Ethical Use of Emerging Technologies:** Radical design ideas often leverage emerging technologies, such as artificial intelligence, biotechnology, and robotics, to create transformative solutions. While these technologies offer immense potential for positive impact, they also raise ethical concerns related to safety, transparency, and accountability. Designers must consider the potential risks and unintended consequences of their ideas and ensure that they adhere to ethical principles and guidelines for responsible innovation.

(b) Navigating Ethical Complexity

Navigating the ethical complexity of radical design ideas requires a multidisciplinary approach that integrates insights from ethics, philosophy, law, and social sciences. Designers must engage in critical reflection, ethical dialogue, and stakeholder engagement to identify and address potential ethical dilemmas, trade-offs, and unintended consequences.

Moreover, designers must adopt a proactive approach to ethical design, integrating ethical considerations into every stage of the design process, from ideation and conceptualization to implementation and evaluation. By incorporating ethical frameworks, guidelines, and best practices into their work, designers can ensure that their radical design ideas uphold principles of fairness, integrity, and social responsibility.

Briefly, the consideration of ethical implications is essential for the responsible development and implementation of radical design ideas. By addressing ethical concerns proactively and transparently, designers can harness the transformative power of innovation to create solutions that benefit society, protect the environment, and uphold fundamental human values and rights. With the clear engagement of stakeholders, and conducting thorough ethical assessments, designers can navigate the complex ethical landscape of radical design concepts and ensure that their creations contribute to a more just, equitable, and sustainable future.

As we push the boundaries of design, let us do so with integrity, empathy, and a commitment to ethical excellence, ensuring that our radical ideas contribute to a future that is just, sustainable, and equitable for all in which our designs serve the greater good and contribute positively to society.

9

Balancing form and function

In the world of design, the interplay between form and function is a fundamental consideration that shapes the success and effectiveness of a design solution. This chapter embarks on an analytical journey to explore the intricate relationship between form and function in design, delving into the principles, challenges, and innovations that underpin this dynamic balance.

9.1 Analysis of the Relationship between Form and Function in Design

Form and function are two essential aspects of design that must harmonize to create meaningful and impactful solutions. At its core, form refers to the visual and aesthetic qualities of a design, encompassing elements such as shape, color, texture, and composition. Function, on the other hand, pertains to the practical purpose or utility of a design, focusing on how well it serves its intended purpose and meets the needs of users.

One of the key principles of design is that form follows function, meaning that the visual appearance of a design should be dictated by its intended use and function. This principle, often attributed to the modernist architect Louis Sullivan, underscores the importance of prioritizing functionality and usability in design while recognizing the role of form in enhancing user experience and aesthetic appeal.

The approach employed involves scrutinizing architectural theories to discern the correlation between Function and Form, exploring:

a. Whether Form follows Function;

b. Whether Function follows Form;

c. Whether Form and Function intertwine.

The interplay between Function and Form defines the essence of the architectural piece. It's concluded that in architectural design, there exists no rigid dictum dictating whether Function precedes Form, Form precedes Function, or they evolve concurrently. Rather, the interrelation between Function and Form amalgamates into a unified approach toward expressing architectural Form. Consequently, observers interpret this Function-Form dynamic as integral to the architectural creation itself. This study's findings advocate for architectural designers to have flexibility in navigating the Function-Form relationship. However, it underscores that the expression of Form must authentically reflect the intended relationship, ensuring that meaning is encapsulated within the architectural creation.

Although in all the conditions the following points should be taken into consideration about the close knit dependency of form and function.

- *Form Follows Function:* One of the fundamental principles in design is the idea that form should follow function. This principle, coined by architect Louis Sullivan, emphasizes the importance of prioritizing functionality and usability in design. According to this philosophy, the aesthetic qualities of a design should emerge organically from its intended purpose and function, rather than being imposed arbitrarily.

- *The Aesthetics of Functionality:* While functionality is paramount, aesthetics play a crucial role in design. A well designed object not only performs its intended function efficiently but also engages the senses, evokes emotion, and enhances the user experience. The challenge for designers is to strike a delicate balance between form and function, ensuring that the visual appeal of a design complements its practical utility without compromising its usability.

- *User - Centered Design:* In today's increasingly user centric approach to design, the needs, preferences, and experiences of end users play a central role in shaping design decisions. User centered design principles advocate for designs that are intuitive, user friendly, and aesthetically pleasing, placing equal emphasis on both form and function. By prioritizing the user experience, designers can create solutions that resonate with users on a deeper level, fostering satisfaction, loyalty, and engagement.

- **Innovative Solutions:** In some cases, innovative solutions emerge when designers challenge traditional notions of form and function. By thinking outside the box and embracing unconventional approaches, designers can create solutions that defy expectations and push the boundaries of what is possible. Whether through biomimicry, where designs are inspired by nature's efficiency and elegance, or through technological innovation, where new materials and manufacturing techniques enable unprecedented forms and functionalities, designers continue to explore new frontiers in balancing form and function.

- **Cultural Influences:** The relationship between form and function is also influenced by cultural factors, historical context, and societal norms. Different cultures may place varying degrees of emphasis on aesthetics versus utility, leading to diverse approaches to design. By celebrating cultural diversity and embracing a global perspective, designers can create solutions that resonate with diverse audiences and reflect the richness of human experience.

The relationship between form and function is a dynamic and multifaceted aspect of design. By understanding the interplay between aesthetic appeal and practical utility, designers can create solutions that are not only visually striking but also highly functional and user friendly. As we continue to explore the balance between form and function in design, we uncover new opportunities for creativity, innovation, and meaningful engagement with the world around us.

However, achieving a harmonious balance between form and function is not always straightforward and requires careful consideration of various factors, including user needs, technological constraints, and cultural context. Designers must navigate a delicate dance between aesthetics and utility, ensuring that their creations not only look beautiful but also perform effectively and efficiently.

9.2 Case Studies Demonstrating Successful Examples of Designs Balancing Aesthetics and Usability

(a) Apple iPhone
The iPhone is a quintessential example of a product that successfully balances form and function. Its sleek, minimalist design is not only visually appealing but also highly functional, with intuitive user interfaces and ergonomic features. From the iconic home button to the seamless integration of hardware and software, every aspect of the iPhone is carefully crafted to enhance both its aesthetic appeal and usability. The result is a device that not only looks beautiful but also feels natural and intuitive to use, making it a beloved and iconic product worldwide.

(b) Vitra Eames Lounge Chair
The Eames Lounge Chair, designed by Charles and Ray Eames for Vitra, is a timeless classic that exemplifies the harmony between form and function. Its elegant, sculptural form is paired with luxurious comfort, making it both a striking piece of furniture and a comfortable seating option. The chair's ergonomic design, premium materials, and meticulous craftsmanship ensure not only its aesthetic appeal but also its practical usability, making it a beloved icon of modern design that continues to be sought after by design enthusiasts around the world.

(c) Tesla Model S
The Tesla Model S is an innovative electric car that combines cutting edge technology with sleek, modern design. Its aerodynamic silhouette, minimalist interior, and high quality finishes create a luxurious and futuristic aesthetic that sets it apart from traditional gasoline powered vehicles. At the same time, the Model S is highly functional, with advanced features such as autopilot, regenerative braking, and over the air software updates that enhance its usability and performance. By seamlessly integrating form and function, Tesla has created a car that not only looks stylish but also delivers an exceptional driving experience.

(d) Dyson Supersonic Hair Dryer
The Dyson Supersonic Hair Dryer is a revolutionary product that redefines the design of a household appliance. Its sleek, futuristic design is not only visually striking but also highly functional, with innovative features such

as intelligent heat control, fast drying technology, and magnetic attachments that enhance its usability and performance. The Supersonic Hair Dryer's ergonomic design, lightweight construction, and user friendly interface make it a joy to use, demonstrating how thoughtful design can elevate everyday products into objects of desire.

(e) Google Pixel Smartphone
The Google Pixel smartphone is renowned for its clean, modern design and intuitive user experience. Its sleek, minimalist exterior belies a wealth of innovative features and capabilities, from its high resolution camera and AI powered software to its seamless integration with Google services. The Pixel's thoughtful design touches, such as its textured power button and colorful accent, add a touch of personality and style while enhancing its usability and appeal. By striking a balance between aesthetics and usability, Google has created a smartphone that not only looks beautiful but also performs flawlessly in everyday use.

These case studies demonstrate how successful designs achieve a harmonious balance between aesthetics and usability. By prioritizing both form and function, designers can create products and experiences that not only delight the senses but also enhance the quality of life for users. As we continue to explore the intersection of aesthetics and usability in design, we uncover new possibilities for innovation, creativity, and humancentered solutions that enrich our lives and elevate the human experience.

9.3 Strategies for designers to prioritize both form and function in their work

Designers face the challenge of balancing aesthetics and usability in their work to create products that are both visually appealing and highly functional. Here are some strategies for designers to prioritize both form and function effectively:

(a) User-Centered Design Approach
Embrace a user-centered design approach that places the needs, preferences, and experiences of end users at the forefront of the design process. Conduct thorough research to gain insights into users' behaviors, motivations, and pain points, and use this information to inform design

decisions. By understanding users' needs and desires, designers can create solutions that resonate with their target audience and deliver exceptional user experiences.

(b) Iterative Design Process
Adopt an iterative design process that allows for continuous refinement and improvement based on user feedback and testing. Prototype early and often to explore different design concepts, gather feedback from stakeholders and end users, and iterate on your designs accordingly. By iterating through multiple design iterations, designers can refine their ideas, identify potential issues, and optimize the balance between form and function.

(c) Design Thinking Methods
Apply design thinking methods such as ideation, prototyping, and testing to explore creative solutions to design challenges. Encourage interdisciplinary collaboration and brainstorming sessions to generate diverse ideas and perspectives. Use prototyping tools and techniques to quickly visualize and test design concepts, allowing for rapid iteration and refinement. By embracing a design thinking mindset, designers can uncover innovative solutions that prioritize both form and function.

(d) Function Driven Design Principles
Prioritize functionality and usability in your designs by adhering to function driven design principles. Start by defining the primary goals and objectives of your design, focusing on solving specific user problems or addressing key user needs. Use principles such as simplicity, clarity, and intuitiveness to guide your design decisions, ensuring that the form of your design is driven by its intended function. Strive to create designs that are intuitive, user friendly, and efficient in fulfilling their intended purpose.

(e) Material and Manufacturing Considerations
Consider the practical constraints of materials and manufacturing processes when designing products. Choose materials and manufacturing techniques that not only enhance the aesthetic appeal of your design but also optimize its functionality and durability. Balance considerations such as cost, sustainability, and manufacturability to ensure that your design is both visually striking and technically feasible.

(f) Feedback and Iteration Loop

Establish a feedback and iteration loop throughout the design process to gather input from stakeholders, end users, and subject matter experts. Solicit feedback early and often, using techniques such as user testing, surveys, and interviews to evaluate the usability and effectiveness of your designs. Incorporate feedback into your design iterations, making adjustments as needed to improve the balance between form and function.

(g) Continuous Learning and Adaptation

Stay informed about emerging trends, technologies, and best practices in design to continuously improve your skills and stay ahead of the curve. Be open to feedback, critique, and constructive criticism, and use it as an opportunity for growth and learning. Remain flexible and adaptable in your approach, willing to iterate and refine your designs based on new insights and changing requirements.

By implementing these strategies, designers can effectively prioritize both form and function in their work, creating products that not only look good but also work well and enhance the lives of their users.

10

Embracing Diversity in Design

In recent years, there has been a growing recognition of the importance of diversity and inclusion in the design industry. Diversity is not only a moral imperative but also a driving force for creativity, innovation, and excellence in the design industry. This chapter advocates for diversity and inclusion in design, emphasizing the importance of embracing diverse perspectives, voices, and experiences to create more inclusive and representative design solutions.

10.1 Advocacy For Diversity and Inclusion in The Design Industry

(a) Promoting Social Equity

Embracing diversity and inclusion in the design industry is fundamentally about promoting social equity and justice. Design has the power to shape our world and influence how people interact with their environments. By ensuring that diverse voices are represented and included in the design process, we can create solutions that are more equitable, accessible, and inclusive for all.

(b) Fostering Creativity and Innovation

Diversity fuels creativity and innovation by bringing together people with different backgrounds, perspectives, and experiences. When individuals from diverse backgrounds collaborate, they bring a variety of ideas, insights, and approaches to problem solving, leading to more innovative and impactful design solutions. By embracing diversity, the design industry can unlock new possibilities, challenge conventional thinking, and drive positive change.

(c) Reflecting Global Perspectives
Design is a global endeavor that reflects the diverse cultures, identities, and experiences of people around the world. Embracing diversity in design allows us to create solutions that resonate with diverse audiences and reflect the richness of human experience. By incorporating diverse perspectives into the design process, we can create products, services, and experiences that are culturally relevant, inclusive, and meaningful to people from all walks of life.

(d) Empowering Underrepresented Voices
In many industries, including design, certain groups have historically been underrepresented or marginalized. Embracing diversity and inclusion is about empowering these underrepresented voices and creating opportunities for them to participate fully in the design process. By providing a platform for diverse designers to share their perspectives, talents, and stories, we can foster a more inclusive and equitable design community.

(e) Driving Economic Growth
Diversity and inclusion are not only ethical imperatives but also drivers of economic growth and competitiveness. Companies that embrace diversity and inclusion tend to be more innovative, resilient, and adaptive to change. By building diverse teams and fostering an inclusive workplace culture, organizations can attract top talent, foster creativity and innovation, and gain a competitive advantage in the marketplace.

(f) Championing Diversity in Design Education
Advocate for diversity and inclusion in design education by promoting a curriculum that reflects diverse perspectives, histories, and cultures. Encouraging collaboration and interdisciplinary learning experiences that expose students to a wide range of design practices and approaches. By championing diversity in design education, we can prepare the next generation of designers to create more inclusive and socially responsible solutions.

(g) Addressing Bias and Discrimination
Address bias and discrimination within the design industry by challenging stereotypes, confronting unconscious biases, and fostering a culture of respect and inclusion. Implement policies and practices that promote diversity, equity, and inclusion in hiring, promotion, and project allocation. By actively addressing bias and discrimination, we can create a more inclusive and supportive work environment for all designers.

(h) Celebrating Diversity in Design Excellence
Celebrating diversity in design excellence by recognizing and showcasing the work of designers from diverse backgrounds and perspectives plays a crucial role in embracing diversity. Highlight projects that demonstrate the power of diversity to drive innovation, creativity, and positive social change. By celebrating diversity in design excellence, we can inspire others to embrace inclusivity and representation in their own work.

Embracing diversity and inclusion in the design industry is essential for promoting social equity, driving innovation, and creating a meaningful impact in the world. By advocating for diversity and inclusion as core principles of design, we can foster a more inclusive and equitable design community that reflects the diversity of the human experience and creates solutions that benefit us all. As we embrace diversity in design, we pave the way for a future that is more inclusive, innovative, and inspiring for generations to come.

10.2 The Benefits of Diverse Perspectives in Design Processes

Diversity is not just a buzzword; it's a fundamental aspect of creating truly innovative and impactful design solutions. This section examines the numerous benefits that diverse perspectives bring to design processes, highlighting how incorporating a wide range of voices and experiences leads to more creative, inclusive, and effective designs.

(a) Enhanced Creativity and Innovation
Diverse perspectives stimulate creativity and innovation by bringing fresh ideas, viewpoints, and approaches to the table. When designers from different backgrounds collaborate, they draw upon a diverse range of experiences, cultural influences, and problem solving strategies, leading to more imaginative and inventive design solutions. By embracing diversity,

design teams can break free from conventional thinking and explore new possibilities that drive innovation forward.

(b) Expanded Problem solving Capabilities
Diverse teams are better equipped to tackle complex design challenges and solve problems creatively. Each team member brings a unique set of skills, knowledge, and perspectives to the table, allowing for a more comprehensive understanding of the problem at hand. By leveraging the diverse expertise of team members, design teams can develop more robust and effective solutions that address a wider range of user needs and preferences.

(c) User-Centered Design
Diversity fosters a deeper understanding of diverse user groups and their needs, preferences, and experiences. When designers from different backgrounds collaborate, they bring insights into the diverse cultural, social, and economic factors that influence user behavior and decision making. This enables design teams to create solutions that are more inclusive, accessible, and user friendly, ensuring that their designs resonate with a broader range of users.

(d) Cultural Relevance and Sensitivity
Diverse perspectives contribute to the cultural relevance and sensitivity of design solutions, ensuring that they are appropriate and respectful of diverse cultural norms, values, and traditions. By incorporating insights from designers with diverse cultural backgrounds, design teams can avoid cultural missteps and create solutions that are meaningful and resonant for users from different cultural backgrounds.

(e) Market Differentiation and Competitive Advantage
Embracing diversity in design processes allows organizations to differentiate themselves in the marketplace and gain a competitive advantage. Design solutions that reflect the diverse needs and preferences of users are more likely to stand out in a crowded market and resonate with target audiences. By prioritizing diversity, organizations can tap into new markets, attract a more diverse customer base, and strengthen their brand reputation as inclusive and socially responsible.

(f) Employee Engagement and Satisfaction

Diversity and inclusion foster a sense of belongingness, respect, and empowerment among employees, leading to higher levels of engagement, satisfaction, and retention. When employees feel valued for their unique perspectives and contributions, they are more motivated to collaborate, innovate, and excel in their work. By fostering a culture of diversity and inclusion, organizations can attract and retain top talent, driving creativity and innovation across the design process.

To sum up, diverse perspectives enrich design processes by enhancing creativity, expanding problem solving capabilities, fostering user-centered design, ensuring cultural relevance and sensitivity, driving market differentiation and competitive advantage, and promoting employee engagement and satisfaction. By embracing diversity in design processes, organizations can create more inclusive, innovative, and impactful design solutions that address the diverse needs and preferences of users around the world.

10.3 Examples of Initiatives and Organizations Promoting Diversity in Design

Across the globe, numerous initiatives and organizations are actively working to promote diversity and inclusivity in the design industry. These initiatives aim to amplify underrepresented voices, foster equitable opportunities, and create more inclusive design practices. Promoting diversity in the design industry requires concerted efforts from individuals, organizations, and communities. Fortunately, there are numerous initiatives and organizations dedicated to advancing diversity and inclusion in design. Here are some inspiring examples:

(a) AIGA Diversity & Inclusion Task Force

The American Institute of Graphic Arts (AIGA) established a Diversity & Inclusion Task Force to address issues of diversity, equity, and inclusion within the design community. The task force collaborates with designers, educators, and industry leaders to develop resources, initiatives, and programs that promote diversity and inclusion in design education, practice, and leadership.

(b) Women Who Design

Women Who Design is a directory of talented women designers, illustrators, and artists from around the world. It is a global network that supports and celebrates women in the design industry. The platform showcases the work of women designers and provides a supportive community for women in the design industry. By highlighting the achievements of women designers, Women Who Design aims to increase the visibility and representation of women in the design field. Through mentorship programs, networking events, and advocacy initiatives, Women in Design aims to empower women designers, address gender disparities in the profession, and promote greater visibility and recognition of women's contributions to design industry.

(c) Black in Design Conference

The Black in Design Conference, organized by the Harvard University Graduate School of Design, is an annual event that celebrates the contributions of Black designers and explores issues of race, identity, and equity in the design profession. The conference features keynote speakers, panel discussions, and workshops focused on promoting diversity and inclusion in design education, practice, discourse, and networking opportunities that promote dialogue and collaboration among Black designers and allies.

(d) The Design Diversity Movement

The Design Diversity Movement is a grassroots initiative that advocates for diversity and inclusion in the design industry. Through workshops, events, and online resources, the movement seeks to empower designers from underrepresented backgrounds, challenge systemic barriers to entry, and promote equity and representation in design education and practice.

(e) Queer Design Club

Queer Design Club is a global community of LGBTQ+ designers and allies working to create a more inclusive and supportive design industry. The club provides a platform for LGBTQ+ designers to connect, share resources, and collaborate on projects. Through events, online forums, and social media initiatives, Queer Design Club amplifies the voices of LGBTQ+ designers and advocates for greater visibility and representation in the design community.

(f) Designing for Diversity Fellowship

The Design for Diversity Fellowship, established by the University of Michigan School of Information, aims to increase diversity and inclusion in the design field. The fellowship provides funding, mentorship, and professional development opportunities for students from underrepresented backgrounds pursuing careers in design research and practice.

(g) Diversity in Design Collaborative

The Diversity in Design Collaborative is a grassroots organization that advocates for greater diversity, equity, and inclusion in the design industry. The collaborative hosts events, workshops, and panel discussions that address issues of representation, accessibility, and social justice in design. Through advocacy and activism, the collaborative seeks to create a more equitable and inclusive design industry for all.

These initiatives and organizations are just a few examples of the many efforts underway to promote diversity and inclusion in the design industry. By supporting and participating in these initiatives, designers can help build a more inclusive and representative design community that reflects the diversity of the world we live in. By collaborating, advocating, and supporting one another, designers can create a more inclusive and representative design industry that reflects the richness and diversity of the world we live in.

11

Celebrating Cultural Influences

Culture is a powerful force that shapes our beliefs, values, and behaviors, influencing every aspect of our lives, including design. In the vibrant world of design and architecture, celebrating cultural influences is a kin to weaving threads of tradition, history, and identity into the very fabric of our built environment. Each culture brings its unique palette of colors, patterns, and motifs, enriching the visual landscape with a kaleidoscope of diversity. From the intricate carvings of ancient temples to the bold geometric shapes of modern skyscrapers, cultural influences infuse architectural marvels with a sense of place and belonging. In design, traditional crafts and artisanal techniques are revitalized, offering a bridge between past and present, while contemporary interpretations breathe new life into age old customs. Whether it's the vibrant hues of Moroccan mosaics, the graceful curves of Japanese pagodas, or the ornate detailing of Indian palaces, cultural influences ignite the imagination, sparking creativity and fostering a deeper appreciation for the world's rich traditions. As we celebrate cultural influences in design and architecture, we not only pay homage to the legacies of the past but also chart a course toward a more inclusive and interconnected future, where diversity is celebrated as the cornerstone of innovation and beauty. This chapter celebrates the rich diversity of cultural influences on design aesthetics and principles, highlighting how different cultural perspectives enrich and inspire design practice.

11.1 Exploration of How Culture Influences Design Aesthetics and Principles

(a) Cultural Identity and Expression

Culture shapes our sense of identity and informs how we express ourselves through design. Cultural symbols, motifs, and traditions often serve as sources of inspiration for designers, influencing the visual language, form, and symbolism of their creations. Whether drawing from indigenous art forms, traditional craftsmanship, or contemporary cultural movements, designers infuse their work with cultural meaning and significance, reflecting the values and aspirations of diverse communities.

(b) Regional Influences and Vernacular Design

Different regions and geographic locations have their own unique design vernaculars, influenced by local customs, climate, materials, and lifestyle. Vernacular architecture, art, and craft traditions provide rich sources of inspiration for designers seeking to create contextually relevant and culturally resonant designs. By embracing regional influences and celebrating local identity, designers can create solutions that are deeply rooted in place and culture, fostering a sense of belonging and connection to the environment.

(c) Cross-Cultural Exchange and Hybridity

In an increasingly interconnected world, cultural influences are constantly evolving and blending through cross-cultural exchange and interaction. Designers draw inspiration from diverse cultural sources, merging elements from different traditions, histories, and aesthetics to create hybrid and multicultural designs. This process of hybridization enriches design practice, fostering innovation, diversity, and creativity by transcending cultural boundaries and fostering new connections and perspectives.

(d) Cultural Sensitivity and Appropriation

While cultural influences can enrich design practice, designers need to approach cross-cultural exchange with sensitivity and respect. Cultural appropriation, the unauthorized or exploitative use of elements from another culture, can perpetuate harmful stereotypes, erode cultural identity, and marginalize indigenous and minority communities. Designers must strive to engage in ethical and responsible practices that honor and respect the cultural origins and meanings of their sources of inspiration, collaborating with communities and stakeholders to ensure that their designs are inclusive, authentic, and culturally sensitive.

(e) Globalization and Cultural Homogenization
As globalization accelerates and cultural boundaries blur, there is a risk of cultural homogenization, where diverse cultural expressions and traditions are overshadowed by dominant global trends and commercial interests. Designers play a critical role in preserving and celebrating cultural diversity by championing local knowledge, skills, and traditions, and advocating for the recognition and preservation of indigenous and minority cultures in the face of globalization pressures.

Culture is a dynamic and multifaceted influence on design aesthetics and principles, shaping our sense of identity, expression, and belonging. By exploring the intersection of culture and design, designers can create solutions that are culturally resonant, contextually relevant, and socially responsible, enriching the human experience and fostering greater understanding and appreciation of our diverse world.

11.2 Case Studies: Designs Inspired by Diverse Cultural Backgrounds

Designers often draw inspiration from a variety of cultural backgrounds, infusing their creations with the richness and diversity of global traditions, histories, and aesthetics. Here are some case studies showcasing examples of designs that celebrate and reflect the rich diversity of cultural influences, highlighting the ways in which designers have incorporated elements from different traditions, histories, and aesthetics into their work.

(a) Ghanaian Kente Cloth Inspired Textiles
One notable example of designs inspired by diverse cultural backgrounds is the use of Ghanaian Kente cloth motifs in textile design. Kente cloth is a traditional Ghanaian textile characterized by its vibrant colors, intricate patterns, and symbolic meanings. Designers around the world have drawn inspiration from Kente cloth motifs to create contemporary textile designs that pay homage to the rich cultural heritage of Ghana while also appealing to modern tastes and sensibilities. These designs often incorporate traditional Kente patterns into contemporary textiles for fashion, home

decor, and accessories, celebrating the beauty and significance of Ghanaian craftsmanship and culture.

(b) Japanese Wabi-Sabi Inspired Architecture
Another example is the use of Japanese wabi-sabi principles in architecture and interior design. Wabi-sabi is a Japanese aesthetic philosophy that celebrates imperfection, impermanence, and the beauty of natural materials. Designers have embraced wabi-sabi principles in their work, incorporating elements such as raw materials, weathered finishes, and minimalist design aesthetics to create spaces that evoke a sense of tranquility, harmony, and authenticity. Drawing inspiration from traditional Japanese architecture and design philosophy, the architect creates a space that embraces simplicity, natural materials, and the beauty of imperfection. The use of natural materials such as wood and stone, as well as the incorporation of elements such as tatami mats and sliding shoji screens, imbues the space with a sense of tranquility and harmony with nature. These designs prioritize simplicity, authenticity, and connection to nature, reflecting the timeless beauty and wisdom of Japanese culture.

(c) African Adinkra Symbol Inspired Jewelry
A fashion designer from Nigeria draws inspiration from the rich cultural heritage of West Africa to create a collection of contemporary clothing. Inspired by traditional African textiles, patterns, and craftsmanship techniques, the designer incorporates bold colors, geometric patterns, and handcrafted embellishments into their designs. Adinkra symbols are a traditional African form of visual communication, representing concepts, proverbs, and philosophical ideas. Designers have been inspired by Adinkra symbols to create contemporary jewelry designs that celebrate African culture and heritage. These designs often feature Adinkra symbols engraved or embossed on metal or incorporated into beaded or woven jewelry pieces. By wearing Adinkra inspired jewelry, individuals can celebrate their African heritage, connect with their cultural roots, and express their identity and values through fashion.

(d) Latin American Inspired Graphic Design
A graphic designer from Brazil explores the visual language of Latin American culture in the design of a branding campaign. Drawing inspiration from indigenous art forms, folk traditions, and vibrant street

culture, the designer creates a dynamic visual identity that reflects the energy, diversity, and vitality of Latin America. Bold colors, playful typography, and expressive illustrations capture the spirit of the region and resonate with audiences both locally and globally.

(e) Mexican Talavera Tile Inspired Patterns

Talavera pottery is a traditional Mexican craft characterized by its colorful hand painted designs and intricate patterns. Designers have been inspired by Talavera tile patterns to create contemporary designs for ceramics, textiles, and home decor accessories. These designs often feature bold colors, geometric motifs, and floral patterns that pay homage to the rich cultural heritage of Mexico while also adding a modern twist. By incorporating Talavera inspired patterns into their work, designers celebrate the vibrant colors, patterns, and craftsmanship of Mexican culture, bringing a touch of Mexico's rich artistic tradition to global audiences.

(f) Islamic Inspired Architecture

An architect from Morocco draws inspiration from Islamic art and architecture in the design of a mosque. Incorporating geometric patterns, intricate arabesques, and traditional architectural elements such as domes and minarets, the architect creates a space that reflects the spiritual and cultural significance of Islam. The use of natural light, symmetry, and ornamentation creates a sense of serenity and reverence, inviting worshippers to connect with the divine.

(g) Indigenous Aboriginal Art Inspired Prints

Aboriginal art is a rich and diverse artistic tradition that spans thousands of years and encompasses a wide range of styles, techniques, and cultural practices. Designers have drawn inspiration from Indigenous Australian art to create contemporary prints and patterns for fashion, textiles, and home decor. These designs often feature bold colors, intricate patterns, and symbolic motifs that pay homage to the spiritual and cultural significance of Aboriginal art. By incorporating Aboriginal art inspired prints into their work, designers celebrate the richness and diversity of Indigenous Australian culture, raising awareness of Indigenous issues and promoting cultural exchange and appreciation.

These case studies demonstrate the power of cultural influences in inspiring innovative and culturally resonant designs that celebrate the richness and diversity of our global heritage. By drawing inspiration from diverse cultural backgrounds, designers can create designs that are not only aesthetically compelling but also meaningful, authentic, and socially responsible, enriching the human experience and fostering greater understanding and appreciation of our shared cultural heritage.

11.3 Cultural Sensitivity and Authenticity in Design: Navigating Ethical and Responsible Practices

Cultural sensitivity and authenticity are essential considerations in design, ensuring that designs respect and honor the cultural heritage, values, and identities of the communities they represent. This section explores the significance of cultural sensitivity and authenticity in design practice and highlights the importance of approaching cross-cultural design with respect, empathy, and integrity.

Understanding Cultural Sensitivity in Design

(a) Respecting Cultural Context

Cultural sensitivity in design begins with a deep respect for the cultural context from which one draws inspiration. Designers must take the time to learn about the cultural traditions, values, and meanings associated with the elements they wish to incorporate into their designs. This includes understanding the historical significance, social context, and cultural symbolism behind cultural artifacts, motifs, and practices.

(b) Avoiding Stereotypes and Appropriation

Designers must be vigilant in avoiding cultural stereotypes and tropes that perpetuate harmful stereotypes or misrepresentations of cultural identities. Cultural appropriation, the unauthorized or exploitative use of elements from another culture, can perpetuate harmful stereotypes, erode cultural identity, and marginalize indigenous and minority communities. Designers must strive to engage in ethical and responsible practices that honor and respect the cultural origins and meanings of their sources of inspiration, collaborating with communities and stakeholders to ensure that their designs are inclusive, authentic, and culturally sensitive.

(c) Engaging in Meaningful Dialogue

Designers should engage in meaningful dialogue and collaboration with members of the communities from which they draw inspiration. This includes seeking input, feedback, and guidance from cultural experts, community leaders, and representatives to ensure that their designs are respectful, accurate, and appropriate. By fostering open and inclusive communication, designers can build trust and mutual respect with the communities they seek to represent, leading to more authentic and culturally sensitive design outcomes.

Embracing Authenticity in Design

(a) Honoring Cultural Heritage

Authenticity in design requires a genuine commitment to honoring and preserving cultural heritage. Designers should approach cultural influences with humility, reverence, and a willingness to learn from the traditions, craftsmanship, and wisdom of diverse cultural communities. By acknowledging and respecting the cultural origins and significance of their sources of inspiration, designers can create designs that are rooted in authenticity and integrity.

(b) Celebrating Diversity and Representation

Authentic design celebrates diversity and representation, reflecting the richness and complexity of human experience. Designers should strive to incorporate diverse perspectives, voices, and experiences into their designs, ensuring that they are inclusive, accessible, and representative of the diverse communities they serve. By celebrating cultural diversity and embracing inclusivity, designers can create designs that resonate with a broader range of users and foster a sense of belonging and connection.

(c) Promoting Social Responsibility

Authentic design is socially responsible, prioritizing the well being and dignity of all individuals and communities. Designers should consider the social, environmental, and ethical implications of their design decisions, striving to create solutions that are sustainable, equitable, and beneficial for society as a whole. By promoting social responsibility and ethical design practices, designers can use their creative talents to address pressing social issues, promote positive social change, and build a more just and compassionate world.

Cultural sensitivity in design entails an ethical responsibility to uphold the dignity, autonomy, and rights of cultural communities. Designers should approach cross-cultural design with integrity, transparency, and accountability, ensuring that their designs are ethically sourced, produced, and marketed. By adhering to ethical standards and best practices, designers can avoid exploitative practices and contribute to the empowerment and self determination of cultural communities, promoting social justice and equity in design.

In summary, cultural sensitivity and authenticity are foundational principles that guide ethical and responsible design practice. By approaching cross-cultural design with respect, empathy, and integrity, designers can create designs that honor and celebrate the rich diversity of human culture, fostering understanding, appreciation, and harmony in an increasingly globalized world. As custodians of culture, designers have a unique opportunity and responsibility to use their creative talents to bridge cultural divides, promote cross-cultural dialogue, and contribute to the creation of a more inclusive, equitable, and harmonious society.

12

Promoting Inclusivity in Design Practices

In an increasingly diverse and interconnected world, the need for inclusivity in design practices has never been greater. In today's rapidly evolving world, designing for accessibility and inclusivity has become not only a moral imperative but also a strategic priority for designers across various industries. This chapter focuses on the crucial discussion of designing with accessibility and inclusivity in mind, exploring the importance of creating products, services, and environments that are accessible to everyone, regardless of their abilities, backgrounds, or identities.

12.1 Designing for Accessibility and Inclusivity: A Critical Imperative

Designing for accessibility and inclusivity is not just a design challenge it's a moral imperative and an opportunity to create a more just, equitable, and inclusive world for everyone. By embracing the principles of accessibility and inclusivity, designers can break down barriers, promote equity, and empower individuals to fully participate in society. Together, we can build a more accessible, inclusive, and welcoming world-one design at a time.

The clear understanding of accessibility and inclusivity in design is a key factor in the marketplace.

Accessibility and inclusivity are closely intertwined concepts that aim to ensure that products, services, and environments are usable and welcoming to people of all abilities, backgrounds, and identities. Accessibility refers to the design of products, services, and environments that can be accessed and used by people with disabilities, including those with mobility impairments, visual or hearing impairments, cognitive or neurological disabilities, and other conditions that may affect their ability to interact with their surroundings. Accessibility focuses on removing barriers and providing accommodations to ensure that everyone, regardless of their abilities, can fully participate in everyday activities and access the same opportunities as others.

Inclusivity, on the other hand, goes beyond mere accessibility to encompass a broader commitment to diversity, equity, and belonging. Inclusivity seeks to create environments that embrace and celebrate the full range of human diversity, including differences in race, ethnicity, gender, sexual orientation, age, socio-economic status, and more. Inclusive design considers the needs and preferences of diverse user groups and strives to create solutions that are responsive to their unique lived experiences and perspectives.

The Importance of Designing for Accessibility and Inclusivity

Designing for accessibility and inclusivity is not just about compliance with legal requirements or meeting minimum standards it's about creating environments that are truly welcoming and empowering for everyone. Here are some key reasons why designing with accessibility and inclusivity in mind is so important:

(a) Promoting Equity and Social Justice

Access to education, employment, healthcare, transportation, and other essential services is a basic human right. Designing with accessibility and inclusivity in mind promotes equity and social justice by ensuring that everyone has equal access to these opportunities, regardless of their abilities or backgrounds. By breaking down barriers and eliminating discrimination, inclusive design helps to level the playing field and create a more just and equitable society for all.

(b) Fostering Innovation and Creativity

Inclusive design encourages innovation and creativity by challenging designers to think outside the box and consider the needs and preferences of diverse user groups. By embracing the full range of human diversity, designers can uncover new insights, identify unmet needs, and develop innovative solutions that benefit everyone. Inclusive design fosters a culture of creativity, empathy, and collaboration, driving positive change and pushing the boundaries of what is possible in design.

(c) Expanding Market Opportunities

Designing with accessibility and inclusivity in mind can also open up new market opportunities and expand the reach of products and services to a wider audience. By catering to the needs of people with disabilities, aging populations, and other underserved communities, designers can tap into a large and growing market segment with significant purchasing power. Inclusive design not only makes good business sense but also reflects a commitment to serving the needs of all customers, regardless of their abilities or backgrounds.

(d) Enhancing User Experience and Satisfaction

Accessible and inclusive design leads to better user experiences and higher levels of satisfaction for all users. By removing barriers and providing accommodations, designers can create products, services, and environments that are easier to use, more intuitive to navigate, and more enjoyable to interact with. Inclusive design improves usability, functionality, and aesthetics, enhancing the overall quality of life for everyone who interacts with the design.

(e) Building Stronger Communities

Inclusive design fosters a sense of belonging and community by creating environments that are welcoming and inclusive to people of all abilities, backgrounds, and identities. By celebrating diversity and embracing differences, designers can create spaces that bring people together, promote social interaction, and build stronger, more resilient communities. Inclusive design creates opportunities for connection, collaboration, and mutual support, enriching the fabric of society and fostering a culture of inclusivity and belonging.

Inclusive design goes beyond mere accessibility; it's about creating spaces and products that are usable, intuitive, and empowering for people of all abilities. This section explores the principles of inclusive design, emphasizing the importance of considering diverse needs and perspectives throughout the design process. By designing with inclusivity in mind from the outset, designers can create solutions that accommodate a wide range of users and foster a sense of belongingness and dignity for all.

Universal design principles guide designers in creating environments and products that are accessible to everyone, regardless of age, ability, or circumstance. From curb cuts and ramps to adjustable furniture and sensory friendly spaces, universal design features benefit not only people with disabilities but also older adults, parents with young children, and anyone else who may encounter barriers in their daily lives. By incorporating universal design principles into their work, designers can create solutions that are flexible, adaptable, and inclusive by design.

Neurodiversity is a concept that recognizes and celebrates the natural variation in human cognition and behavior. Designing for neurodiversity involves creating environments and products that accommodate the diverse sensory, cognitive, and emotional needs of individuals with conditions such as autism, ADHD, and sensory processing disorders. From quiet spaces and sensory friendly lighting to visual schedules and interactive installations, designers can create inclusive environments that support the unique strengths and challenges of neurodiverse individuals, fostering a sense of comfort, safety, and belonging for all.

User-centered design processes prioritize the needs and experiences of diverse users, involving them in every stage of the design process from research and ideation to prototyping and testing. By actively engaging with users and stakeholders, designers can gain valuable insights into their needs, preferences, and lived experiences, ensuring that their designs are responsive, intuitive, and inclusive. Whether through participatory design workshops, co-creation sessions, or user testing sessions, involving diverse voices in the design process is essential for creating solutions that truly meet the needs of all users.

In the bustling streets of a major city, inclusive urban design features such as curb cuts, tactile paving, and audible pedestrian signals ensure that people of all abilities can navigate the built environment safely and independently. By incorporating universal design principles into public spaces, cities can create environments that are welcoming and accessible to everyone, promoting social inclusion and civic engagement for all residents and visitors.

In the modern workplace, inclusive design features such as adjustable desks, ergonomic seating, and quiet zones support the diverse needs of employees with varying abilities and preferences. By creating flexible and adaptable work environments, companies can empower employees to work more comfortably and efficiently, boosting productivity, morale, and retention rates. Inclusive workplace design also sends a powerful message of diversity and inclusion, fostering a culture of belonging and respect for all employees.

In the digital age, technology has the power to break down barriers and create new opportunities for inclusion. Accessible technology solutions such as screen readers, voice recognition softwares, and alternative input devices enable people with disabilities to access digital content and interact with devices more effectively. By designing technologies with accessibility in mind, companies can reach a broader audience, enhance user experiences, and promote digital equity and inclusion for all.

Inclusive educational environments provide a supportive and inclusive learning environment for students of all abilities. From accessible classrooms and assistive technology to inclusive teaching practices and peer support programs, inclusive education design fosters a sense of being at the right place and academic success for all students. By creating environments where every student can thrive, schools and educational institutions can promote social inclusion, diversity, and equity in education.

Briefly, "Promoting Inclusivity in Design Practices: Crafting Spaces for All" is a call to action for designers to embrace inclusivity as a guiding principle in their work. By designing with empathy, creativity, and a commitment to diversity and equity, designers can create environments and products that are accessible, welcoming, and empowering for everyone. From urban streetscapes and workplace environments to digital interfaces and educational settings, inclusive design has the power to transform lives, promote social inclusion, and build a more just and equitable society for all.

12.2 Examples of inclusive design practices that consider diverse user needs

Inclusive design practices aim to create products, environments, and experiences that consider the diverse needs of users, ensuring accessibility, usability, and inclusivity for everyone. Let's explore some inspiring examples of inclusive design practices that have successfully addressed diverse user needs:

(a) Microsoft's Xbox Adaptive Controller

Microsoft's Xbox Adaptive Controller is a groundbreaking example of inclusive design in the gaming industry. Designed to meet the needs of gamers with limited mobility, the controller features large programmable buttons, customizable inputs, and compatibility with a wide range of external adaptive switches and accessories. By allowing users to customize their gaming experience according to their unique abilities and preferences, the Xbox Adaptive Controller promotes accessibility and inclusivity in gaming, enabling more people to participate and enjoy the immersive world of video games. Microsoft aims to create products and services that are accessible and empowering for everyone, regardless of their abilities or limitations.

(b) IKEA's OMTÄNKSAM Collection

IKEA's OMTÄNKSAM collection is a line of furniture and accessories designed with the needs of older adults and people with disabilities in mind. From ergonomic chairs and easy grip utensils to nonslip rugs and adjustable lighting, the OMTÄNKSAM collection features thoughtful design solutions that enhance comfort, safety, and accessibility in the home. By incorporating universal design principles into their products, IKEA promotes inclusivity and independence for users of all ages and abilities, enabling them to live more comfortably and confidently in their living spaces.

(c) IKEA's "ThisAbles" Initiative

IKEA's "ThisAbles" initiative is a prime example of inclusive design in action. In collaboration with disability organizations and activists, IKEA developed a range of 3D printed accessories that can be added to existing IKEA furniture to make them more accessible to people with disabilities. These accessories include easy to grip handles, extended legs for raising furniture height, and large buttoned light switches, among others. By offering these accessories as free downloadable files, IKEA empowers customers to customize their furniture to meet their unique needs, promoting independence and inclusion for people of all abilities.

(d) Oxo Good Grips Kitchen Tools
Oxo Good Grips is renowned for its line of kitchen tools that are designed with accessibility and usability in mind. Featuring soft, nonslip handles, oversized grips, and intuitive ergonomic shapes, Oxo's kitchen tools are easy to hold and manipulate for people with limited dexterity or strength. These design features benefit not only people with disabilities but also older adults, children, and anyone else who may encounter challenges in the kitchen. By prioritizing user friendly design, Oxo demonstrates how inclusive design practices can enhance usability and enjoyment for all users.

(e) Airbnb's Accessibility Features
Airbnb's commitment to inclusivity extends beyond its platform to include a range of accessibility features designed to meet the needs of travelers with disabilities. From searchable filters for accessible listings to detailed accessibility information and photos, Airbnb's platform enables users to find and book accommodations that meet their specific needs and preferences. By prioritizing accessibility and transparency, Airbnb promotes inclusivity in travel and hospitality, empowering travelers with disabilities to explore new destinations and enjoy memorable experiences around the world.

(f) Google's Live Caption Feature
Google's Live Caption feature is a powerful accessibility tool that provides real time captions for videos and audio content on Android devices. Designed to support users who are deaf or hard of hearing, Live Caption uses advanced speech recognition technology to generate accurate captions for any media playing on the device, including videos, podcasts, and phone calls. By enabling users to access spoken content in written form, Live Caption promotes accessibility and inclusion in digital

communication, allowing users to engage more fully with the world around them. By integrating Live Caption into its operating system, Google demonstrates its commitment to making technology more inclusive and accessible for everyone.

(g) Nike's FlyEase Sneakers

Nike's FlyEase sneakers are a prime example of inclusive design in the footwear industry. Featuring a hands free entry system and adjustable closures, FlyEase sneakers are designed to be easy to put on and take off, making them accessible to people of all ages and abilities, including those with limited dexterity or mobility. By prioritizing ease of use and accessibility without compromising on style or performance, Nike's FlyEase sneakers promote inclusivity and independence for wearers, empowering them to move confidently and comfortably in their everyday lives.

(h) Citymapper's Accessible Routing Options

Citymapper, a popular navigation app, offers accessible routing options designed to meet the needs of users with mobility challenges. By providing detailed information on wheelchair accessible routes, step free entrances, and accessible public transportation options, Citymapper helps users plan their journeys more efficiently and confidently, ensuring that they can navigate the city with ease and independence. By prioritizing accessibility and inclusivity in its navigation features, Citymapper promotes equal access to transportation and urban mobility for all users, regardless of their mobility limitations.

(i) The High Line

The High Line in New York City is a public park built on a historic elevated railway line. Designed with accessibility in mind, the High Line features gently sloping pathways, wide entrances, and ample seating areas that accommodate people of all ages and abilities. The park's accessible design enables wheelchair users, parents with strollers, and people with mobility aids to navigate the space comfortably and independently, promoting social inclusion and civic engagement for all residents and visitors.

These examples illustrate the power of inclusive design practices to promote accessibility, equity, and inclusion for diverse users. By considering the needs and perspectives of all users throughout the design process, designers can create products, environments, and services that are truly inclusive and empowering for everyone, regardless of their abilities or limitations.

12.3 Strategies for incorporating inclusivity into the design process from the outset

Incorporating inclusivity into the design process from the outset is essential for creating products, services, and environments that are accessible and welcoming to people of all abilities, backgrounds, and identities. Here are some strategies for designers to consider when striving to make inclusivity a central focus of their work:

(a) User-Centered Design Approach

Adopt a user-centered design approach that prioritizes understanding the needs, preferences, and experiences of diverse user groups. Conduct research, surveys, interviews, and usability testing to gather insights into the barriers and challenges faced by users with different abilities, cultural backgrounds, and identities. By involving users in the design process from the outset, designers can ensure that their solutions are truly responsive to the needs and preferences of the people they serve.

(b) Inclusive Design Principles

Embrace inclusive design principles that guide the development of products, services, and environments that are accessible and usable by people of all abilities. Some key principles of inclusive design include flexibility, simplicity, clarity, and responsiveness to user needs. Designers should strive to create solutions that accommodate a wide range of abilities, preferences, and contexts, avoiding one size fits all approaches that may exclude or marginalize certain users.

(c) Diverse Design Teams

Build diverse design teams that bring together individuals with a variety of backgrounds, perspectives, and lived experiences. Diversity fosters creativity, innovation, and empathy, enabling teams to identify and address a broader range of user needs and preferences. By fostering a culture of inclusion and collaboration, design teams can create solutions that reflect the diversity of the communities they serve, promoting equity and representation in the design process.

(d) Accessibility Guidelines and Standards
Familiarize yourself with accessibility guidelines and standards, such as the Web Content Accessibility Guidelines (WCAG) and the Americans with Disabilities Act (ADA) standards. These guidelines provide practical recommendations and best practices for designing accessible digital interfaces, physical environments, and communication materials. By adhering to accessibility standards, designers can ensure that their solutions meet the needs of users with disabilities and comply with legal and regulatory requirements.

(e) Early Prototyping and Iteration
Incorporate inclusivity into the design process from the earliest stages by prototyping and iterating designs based on user feedback and testing. Start with low fidelity prototypes that allow for quick experimentation and refinement, soliciting feedback from diverse user groups at each stage of development. Iterate on designs based on user input, making adjustments and improvements to address usability issues, accessibility barriers, and user preferences. By involving users early and often, designers can identify and resolve potential issues before they become entrenched in the final product.

(f) Inclusive Language and Imagery
Use inclusive language and imagery throughout the design process to ensure that your communications are respectful, inclusive, and representative of diverse identities and experiences. Avoid language or imagery that may perpetuate stereotypes, stigmatize marginalized groups, or exclude certain individuals. Instead, strive to use language and imagery that reflect the diversity of your audience, promoting a sense of belonging and inclusivity for all users.

(g) Continuous Learning and Improvement
Commitment to continuous learning and improvement by staying informed about emerging trends, research findings, and best practices in inclusive design. Attend workshops, conferences, and training sessions on

accessibility, diversity, and inclusion to expand your knowledge and skills. Engage with communities and organizations that promote inclusivity in design, seeking opportunities to collaborate, share insights, and learn from others. By remaining open minded and receptive to feedback, designers can continuously evolve and refine their approach to inclusivity, driving positive change in their practice and the broader design community.

Incorporation of these strategies into their design process, designers can create products, services, and environments that are truly inclusive, accessible, and empowering for people of all abilities, backgrounds, and identities. By prioritizing inclusivity from the outset, designers can contribute to a more equitable and inclusive society, where everyone has the opportunity to participate fully and thrive.

13

Championing Eco-Friendly Designs

In the quest for sustainable living, championing eco-friendly designs emerges as a beacon of hope amid environmental concerns. This chapter explores the transformative power of conscious design, where every blueprint, material choice, and construction method holds the potential to mitigate ecological footprints. From architectural marvels that seamlessly integrate with nature to everyday objects crafted from recycled materials, the spectrum of eco-friendly designs is as diverse as it is innovative. Through meticulous attention to detail and a commitment to harmonize human needs with the planet's well being, designers become stewards of change, reshaping industries and inspiring a global shift towards a greener future.

13.1 Advocacy for Environmentally Sustainable Design Practices

In today's world, where environmental concerns are at the forefront of global consciousness, advocating for environmentally sustainable design practices is not just a choice but a necessity. This chapter explains the importance of championing eco-friendly designs and the role designers play in promoting environmental stewardship through their creative work.

(a) Environmental Awareness and Responsibility

The activism for environmentally sustainable design practices begins with raising awareness about the environmental impact of design decisions and the urgent need for sustainable alternatives. Designers have a responsibility to educate themselves and others about the environmental challenges we face, from climate change and resource depletion to pollution and habitat destruction. By understanding the interconnectedness of human activity and the natural world, designers can advocate for more responsible and regenerative design practices that minimize harm to the environment and promote ecological resilience.

(b) Ethical Imperative and Moral Obligation
There is an ethical imperative and moral obligation for designers to prioritize environmental sustainability in their work. As creators and innovators, designers have the power to influence the choices and behaviors of individuals, organizations, and societies at large. By advocating for eco-friendly designs, designers can help shift the paradigm towards a more sustainable and equitable future for all living beings. This requires designers to question the status quo, challenge unsustainable practices, and champion alternative approaches that prioritize environmental stewardship, social responsibility, and economic viability.

(c) Regenerative Design Principles
Working towards environmentally sustainable design practices involves embracing regenerative design principles that go beyond minimizing harm to actively restoring and enhancing ecological health and vitality. Designers should seek to create designs that mimic natural systems, processes, and patterns, promoting resource efficiency, biodiversity, and resilience. By integrating principles of biomimicry, permaculture, and circular economy into their designs, designers can contribute to the regeneration of ecosystems, communities, and cultures, fostering a more harmonious and symbiotic relationship between humans and the natural world.

(d) Collaborative Partnerships and Collective Action
Encouraging eco-friendly designs requires collaborative partnerships and collective action among designers, industry stakeholders, policymakers, and communities. Designers should collaborate with experts in environmental science, engineering, and ecology to incorporate sustainability principles into their designs effectively. They should also engage with clients, suppliers, and manufacturers to promote sustainable

sourcing, production, and distribution practices throughout the supply chain. By working together towards shared goals and objectives, designers can amplify their impact and drive meaningful change at scale.

(e) Education and Empowerment
Advocating for environmentally sustainable design practices involves educating and empowering the next generation of designers to be stewards of the environment and agents of change. Design schools and programs should integrate sustainability principles into their curricula, teaching students about the environmental impact of design decisions and equipping them with the knowledge, skills, and tools needed to create eco-friendly designs. Designers should also mentor and support emerging talent, providing opportunities for hands-on learning, real world experience, and professional development in sustainable design practices.

(f) Public Awareness and Engagement
Advocating for eco-friendly designs requires raising public awareness and mobilizing collective action to address pressing environmental challenges. Designers can use their platforms and influence to communicate environmental issues effectively, inspire action, and mobilize support for sustainable solutions. Through design exhibitions, public installations, and multimedia campaigns, designers can engage audiences in meaningful conversations about sustainability, encouraging them to make informed choices and adopt more environmentally friendly behaviors in their daily lives.

Promoting environmentally sustainable design practices is essential for addressing the urgent environmental challenges we face and building a more sustainable and resilient future for generations to come. By championing eco-friendly designs, designers can harness the power of creativity, innovation, and collaboration to protect and preserve the natural world, promote social equity, and create a world where people and planet thrive in harmony.

13.2 Examination of the Environmental Impact of Design Processes and Products

Understanding the environmental impact of design processes and products is crucial for promoting eco-friendly practices and mitigating harm to the planet. This section examines the various ways in which design can affect the environment and highlights the importance of adopting sustainable approaches to minimize negative consequences.

(a) Resource Consumption and Depletion
One of the primary environmental impacts of design processes is resource consumption and depletion. From raw materials extraction to manufacturing, transportation, and disposal, every stage of the design lifecycle requires significant amounts of energy, water, and natural resources. This can lead to the depletion of finite resources such as fossil fuels, minerals, and fresh water, as well as the degradation of ecosystems and habitats through land use change, deforestation, and pollution. Designers must consider the environmental implications of their material choices, production methods, and supply chain management to minimize resource consumption and promote resource efficiency and conservation.

(b) Energy Use and Greenhouse Gas Emissions
Design processes and products also contribute to greenhouse gas emissions and climate change through the consumption of energy and the release of carbon dioxide and other greenhouse gases into the atmosphere. Energy intensive manufacturing processes, transportation logistics, and end of life disposal methods all contribute to carbon emissions, exacerbating global warming and climate instability. Designers should prioritize energy efficiency, renewable energy sources, and low carbon manufacturing techniques to reduce their carbon footprint and mitigate climate impacts. By embracing renewable energy technologies, optimizing energy use, and minimizing waste generation, designers can help transition to a low carbon economy and mitigate the worst effects of climate change.

(c) Waste Generation and Pollution
Another significant environmental impact of design processes and products is waste generation and pollution. Design manufacturing generates vast quantities of waste, including solid waste, wastewater, and hazardous chemicals, which can contaminate air, water, and soil, posing serious risks to human health and the environment. Designers must adopt waste reduction strategies such as waste minimization, recycling, and closed loop manufacturing to prevent pollution and conserve resources. By designing products with longevity, durability, and recyclability in mind,

designers can reduce the need for raw materials extraction, extend product lifecycles, and minimize waste generation throughout the design lifecycle.

(d) Biodiversity Loss and Habitat Destruction
Design activities can also contribute to biodiversity loss and habitat destruction through land use change, habitat fragmentation, and ecosystem degradation. The extraction of raw materials, such as timber, minerals, and metals, can disrupt natural ecosystems, destroy critical habitats, and threaten biodiversity hotspots. Designers should prioritize sustainable sourcing, responsible forestry practices, and habitat restoration initiatives to protect biodiversity and preserve ecosystem services. By promoting biodiversity conservation and ecosystem restoration, designers can help safeguard the planet's natural capital and ensure the well being of future generations.

(e) Water Pollution and Scarcity
Design processes and products can also impact water resources through pollution and overconsumption. Industrial manufacturing, agriculture, and urban development generate pollution that contaminates water bodies, degrades water quality, and threatens aquatic ecosystems and human health. Additionally, water intensive manufacturing processes, such as textile dyeing and leather tanning, can exacerbate water scarcity in water stressed regions, exacerbating social and environmental inequalities. Designers should prioritize water efficiency, pollution prevention, and water stewardship practices to minimize their water footprint and protect freshwater ecosystems. By adopting water saving technologies, implementing water recycling and reuse systems, and supporting community based water management initiatives, designers can help conserve water resources and promote water security for all.

Examining the environmental impact of design processes and products is essential for promoting sustainability and mitigating harm to the planet. By understanding the interconnections between design activities and environmental outcomes, designers can identify opportunities to reduce resource consumption, minimize pollution, and protect natural ecosystems and biodiversity. Through holistic lifecycle assessments, transparent supply chain management, and stakeholder engagement, designers can adopt sustainable approaches that prioritize environmental stewardship, social responsibility, and economic viability, paving the way for a more sustainable and resilient future for all.

13.3 Examples of Eco-Friendly Design Solutions Prioritizing Sustainability

Eco-friendly design solutions prioritize sustainability by minimizing environmental impact, conserving resources, and promoting responsible stewardship of the planet. Here are some detailed examples of eco-friendly design solutions across various industries:

(a) Biophilic Architecture

Biophilic architecture incorporates natural elements and features into building design to enhance occupant well being and minimize environmental impact. Examples include green roofs and walls, which reduce energy consumption, mitigate urban heat island effects, and provide habitats for wildlife. Additionally, daylighting strategies maximize natural light penetration, reducing the need for artificial lighting and improving indoor air quality. Biophilic architecture fosters a connection to nature, promotes biodiversity, and enhances the overall sustainability of built environments.

(b) Cradle-to-Cradle Design

Cradle-to-cradle design approaches aim to create products and systems that are regenerative by design, with materials and components that can be continually recycled, reused, or composted at the end of their life cycle. Examples include products made from biodegradable or recyclable materials, such as bioplastics, bamboo, and reclaimed wood. By adopting cradle-to-cradle principles, designers can minimize waste generation, conserve resources, and promote circular economies that prioritize sustainability and resilience.

(c) Zero-Energy Buildings

Zero-energy buildings generate as much renewable energy as they consume over the course of a year, minimizing carbon emissions and energy costs while maximizing energy efficiency and occupant comfort. Examples include passive solar design strategies, such as orientation, insulation, and thermal mass, which optimize solar gain and minimize heat loss. Additionally, renewable energy technologies such as solar panels, wind turbines, and geothermal heat pumps can further reduce energy consumption and promote self sufficiency. Zero-energy buildings demonstrate the potential for sustainable architecture to mitigate climate change, enhance resilience, and improve quality of life for occupants.

(d) Sustainable Fashion

Sustainable fashion encompasses design practices that prioritize environmental, social, and economic sustainability throughout the entire supply chain, from sourcing to production, distribution, and end of life disposal. Examples include eco-friendly materials such as organic cotton, hemp, and recycled polyester, which reduce water consumption, chemical use, and greenhouse gas emissions compared to conventional materials. Additionally, slow fashion principles such as durability, repairability, and timeless design promote longevity and reduce textile waste. Sustainable fashion initiatives aim to transform the industry by promoting transparency, ethical labor practices, and conscious consumer behavior.

(e) Permaculture Design

Permaculture design integrates ecological principles and systems thinking to create sustainable and resilient human habitats that mimic natural ecosystems. Examples include food forests, which combine fruit and nut trees, perennial vegetables, and herbs to create productive and biodiverse landscapes that provide food, fuel, fiber, and medicine while enhancing soil fertility and ecosystem health. Additionally, rainwater harvesting systems capture and store water for irrigation, reducing dependence on municipal water supplies and promoting water self sufficiency. Permaculture design fosters regenerative agriculture, community resilience, and ecological restoration, offering holistic solutions to environmental challenges.

(f) Green Transportation Design

Green transportation design focuses on reducing emissions, energy consumption, and environmental impact while maximizing efficiency, accessibility, and safety. Examples include electric vehicles (EVs) powered by renewable energy sources such as solar, wind, and hydropower, which eliminate tailpipe emissions and reduce air pollution and greenhouse gas emissions. Additionally, active transportation infrastructure such as bike lanes, pedestrian walkways, and public transit systems promote sustainable mobility and reduce traffic congestion and carbon emissions. Green transportation design prioritizes clean, affordable, and equitable transportation options that enhance quality of life and protect the planet.

(g) Sustainable Product Design

Sustainable product design integrates lifecycle thinking, material innovation, and circular economy principles to create products that are environmentally responsible, socially equitable, and economically viable. Examples include modular furniture systems made from recycled and recyclable materials, which allow for easy disassembly, repair, and reuse at the end of their life cycle. Additionally, product-as-a-service (PaaS) models enable consumers to lease or share products rather than own them outright, reducing resource consumption, waste generation, and environmental impact. Sustainable product design fosters a culture of responsible consumption, resource efficiency, and environmental stewardship, offering innovative solutions to pressing sustainability challenges.

These examples demonstrate the diverse ways in which eco-friendly design solutions prioritize sustainability by minimizing environmental impact, conserving resources, and promoting responsible stewardship of the planet. By adopting sustainable design principles and practices, designers can contribute to a more sustainable, resilient, and equitable future for all.

14

Sustainable Materials and Practices

In the chapter titled "Sustainable Materials and Practices," the foundational principles of eco-conscious design take center stage. Exploring into the heart of sustainable architecture and product development, this chapter explores the intricate balance between human creativity and environmental responsibility. By scrutinizing the lifecycle of materials and practices employed in design processes, readers gain a comprehensive understanding of their ecological impact. Through illuminating case studies and expert insights, this chapter serves as a guiding beacon for aspiring designers and seasoned professionals alike, offering tangible pathways towards incorporating sustainability into every facet of design. From the sourcing of renewable resources to the implementation of innovative construction techniques, "Sustainable Materials and Practices" lays the groundwork for a more conscientious approach to design that honors both present and future generations.

14.1 Exploration of Sustainable Materials and Manufacturing Processes in Design

In recent years, there has been a growing emphasis on sustainability within the design industry, with a focus on adopting eco-friendly materials and manufacturing processes to minimize environmental impact. This exploration explores various sustainable materials and practices used in design, highlighting their benefits and implications for the environment.

Sustainable Materials: Sustainable materials are sourced, produced, and used in ways that minimize environmental impact and promote ecological balance. Some examples include:

- ***Bamboo:*** Bamboo is a fast growing and renewable resource that can be used for various design applications, including furniture, flooring, and textiles. It requires minimal water and pesticides to grow and regenerates quickly, making it an environmentally friendly alternative to traditional wood.

- ***Recycled Materials:*** Recycled materials such as recycled plastic, glass, and metal are repurposed from post-consumer or post-industrial waste, diverting materials from landfills and reducing the need for virgin resources. These materials can be used in a wide range of design applications, including packaging, furniture, and construction.

- ***Cork:*** Cork is a sustainable and renewable material harvested from the bark of cork oak trees. It is lightweight, durable, and biodegradable, making it suitable for a variety of design applications, including flooring, wall coverings, and fashion accessories.

- ***Sustainable Wood:*** Sustainable wood products, certified by organizations such as the Forest Stewardship Council (FSC), are sourced from responsibly managed forests that prioritize biodiversity, conservation, and community engagement. These products are harvested using sustainable forestry practices that minimize habitat destruction, soil erosion, and carbon emissions.

- ***Bioplastics:*** Bioplastics are derived from renewable biomass sources such as plants, algae, and bacteria and are biodegradable or compostable at the end of their life cycle. They offer a more sustainable alternative to traditional petroleum based plastics, which contribute to pollution and resource depletion.

Sustainable Manufacturing Processes: Sustainable manufacturing processes aim to reduce energy consumption, waste generation, and environmental pollution while maximizing resource efficiency and product quality. Some examples include:

- ***Energy Efficient Production:*** Energy efficient manufacturing processes use renewable energy sources such as solar, wind, and hydroelectric power to minimize carbon emissions and reduce reliance on fossil fuels. Technologies such as energy efficient lighting, heating, and cooling systems can also help reduce energy consumption and operating costs.

- *Water Conservation:* Water conservation measures such as rainwater harvesting, wastewater recycling, and water efficient fixtures can help reduce water consumption and minimize pollution of freshwater resources. Additionally, water based paints and coatings can replace solvent based alternatives, reducing harmful emissions and improving indoor air quality.

- *Waste Reduction:* Waste reduction strategies such as lean manufacturing, material recycling, and closed loop production systems can help minimize waste generation and promote resource conservation. By repurposing waste materials and byproducts, manufacturers can reduce landfill disposal and lower raw material costs.

- *Lifecycle Assessment:* Lifecycle assessment (LCA) is a systematic approach to evaluating the environmental impacts of a product or process throughout its entire lifecycle, from raw material extraction to end of life disposal. By quantifying the environmental impacts of design decisions, manufacturers can identify opportunities for improvement and optimize product sustainability.

- *Supply Chain Transparency:* Supply chain transparency initiatives such as fair trade certification, ethical sourcing, and responsible production practices help ensure that materials and products are sourced and manufactured in ways that prioritize social and environmental responsibility. By promoting transparency and accountability, manufacturers can build trust with consumers and stakeholders and support ethical and sustainable practices throughout the supply chain.

Sustainable materials and practices play a crucial role in minimizing environmental impact and promoting ecological balance within the design industry. By adopting eco-friendly materials and manufacturing processes, designers and manufacturers can reduce resource consumption, minimize waste generation, and mitigate pollution, contributing to a more sustainable and resilient future for all. As the demand for sustainable design continues to grow, it is essential for the industry to embrace innovative solutions that prioritize environmental stewardship and promote social responsibility.

14.2 Case Studies: Innovative Uses of Recycled Materials in Design Projects

In recent years, designers and architects have increasingly turned to recycled materials as a sustainable alternative to traditional resources, showcasing innovative and creative ways to repurpose waste into functional and aesthetically pleasing design solutions. The following case studies showcase inspiring examples of how designers have incorporated recycled materials into their projects, demonstrating the potential for sustainable design solutions across various industries.

(a) Plastic Bottle Pavilion

- *Project Overview:* In São Paulo, Brazil, a team of architects and designers collaborated to create a temporary pavilion entirely constructed from recycled plastic bottles. The pavilion served as an interactive art installation and educational space, drawing attention to the issue of plastic waste while demonstrating the potential for recycling and upcycling materials.

- *Design Approach:* The design team collected thousands of plastic bottles from local recycling centers and waste dumps, thoroughly cleaned and sanitized them, and then arranged them in a grid like pattern to form the walls and roof of the pavilion. The translucent bottles allowed natural light to filter through during the day, creating a captivating interplay of light and shadow, while LED lights embedded within the structure illuminated the pavilion at night.

- *Impact:* The plastic bottle pavilion served as a powerful symbol of sustainability and environmental stewardship, inspiring visitors to rethink their consumption habits and consider the potential of recycled materials in design. The project also sparked conversations about waste management and recycling infrastructure in São Paulo, prompting local authorities to explore initiatives to reduce plastic pollution and promote recycling in the city.

(b) Newspaper Chair
- ***Project Overview:*** A furniture designer in Amsterdam created a series of chairs using recycled newspapers as the primary material. The newspaper chairs were designed to be lightweight, durable, and environmentally friendly, showcasing the potential for repurposing waste materials in furniture design.

- ***Design Approach:*** The designer developed a proprietary process for transforming newspapers into a composite material suitable for furniture construction. The newspapers were shredded into small pieces, mixed with a non toxic adhesive, and then molded into chair frames using a custom designed form. The resulting chairs featured a distinctive texture and pattern reminiscent of newsprint, adding a unique aesthetic element to the design.

- ***Impact:*** The newspaper chairs garnered widespread attention for their innovative use of recycled materials and sustainable design principles. They were exhibited at design fairs and galleries around the world, sparking discussions about the potential for upcycling waste materials in furniture manufacturing. The project also inspired other designers and manufacturers to explore similar approaches to sustainable design, contributing to a growing movement towards circular economy practices in the furniture industry.

(c) Glass Bottle Façade
- ***Project Overview:*** In Barcelona, Spain, an architecture firm transformed an abandoned warehouse into a vibrant office space featuring a striking facade made entirely of recycled glass bottles. The glass bottle facade not only provided a visually stunning aesthetic but also served as a functional shading element, reducing solar heat gain and glare within the building.

- ***Design Approach:*** The architects collected discarded glass bottles from local recycling centers and arranged them in a modular grid pattern to form the facade panels. The bottles were held in place with a structural frame made of recycled steel, creating a dynamic interplay of light and color as sunlight filtered through the translucent glass. The facade also incorporated integrated planters for greenery, further enhancing the sustainability and biophilic design elements of the project.

- *Impact:* The glass bottle facade received widespread acclaim for its innovative design and environmental benefits, demonstrating the potential for repurposing waste materials in architectural applications. The project showcased the versatility of recycled glass as a building material and inspired other architects and developers to explore similar approaches to sustainable architecture. Additionally, the use of recycled materials helped reduce the project's carbon footprint and contribute to the circular economy by diverting waste from landfills.

(d) Tire Playground

- *Project Overview:* A landscape architect in Toronto, Canada, transformed a vacant lot into a playful and sustainable community playground using recycled tires as the primary material. The tire playground provided a safe and engaging space for children to explore and interact while promoting environmental awareness and recycling education.

- *Design Approach:* The landscape architect collaborated with local tire recycling facilities to source thousands of discarded tires, which were cleaned, painted, and repurposed into various play structures such as swings, slides, and climbing walls. The tires were arranged in imaginative configurations to encourage creative play and physical activity, with colorful patterns and designs adding visual interest to the space.

- *Impact:* The tire playground quickly became a beloved community gathering space, attracting children and families from the surrounding neighborhood. It provided a sustainable and cost-effective solution for transforming underutilized urban spaces into vibrant recreational areas, promoting social interaction, physical fitness, and environmental stewardship. The project also raised awareness about the importance of recycling and waste reduction, inspiring residents to rethink their attitudes towards discarded materials and explore opportunities for creative reuse in their own communities.

(e) The Eco-Helmet by Isis Shiffer

- **Project Overview:** "The Eco-Helmet by Isis Shiffer" represents a groundbreaking innovation in sustainable design within the realm of urban transportation. Conceived as a response to the pressing need for eco-friendly solutions in bike safety gear, this project aims to revolutionize the conventional helmet design by utilizing recyclable materials and advanced manufacturing techniques. With a focus on affordability and accessibility, the Eco-Helmet seeks to bridge the gap between safety, sustainability, and style, catering to the needs of environmentally conscious commuters worldwide.

- **Design Approach:** At the core of Isis Shiffer's design approach lies a commitment to marrying functionality with environmental responsibility. The Eco-Helmet leverages cutting edge technologies such as 3D printing and biodegradable materials to create a lightweight yet durable head protection solution. By prioritizing aerodynamics and impact resistance, Shiffer ensures that safety standards are not compromised in the pursuit of sustainability. Moreover, the modular design allows for easy assembly and disassembly, facilitating repairs and recycling, thereby extending the product's lifecycle, and minimizing waste.

- **Impact:** The Eco-Helmet's impact reverberates beyond the realm of bike safety gear, serving as a testament to the transformative power of sustainable design. By offering a viable alternative to traditional helmets, Shiffer's creation promotes eco-conscious consumer choices and fosters a culture of environmental stewardship within the cycling community. Furthermore, the widespread adoption of such innovations has the potential to reduce carbon emissions associated with traditional manufacturing processes while simultaneously inspiring future generations of designers to prioritize sustainability in their creations. As a symbol of ingenuity and sustainability, the Eco-Helmet by Isis Shiffer represents a significant step towards a greener, safer, and more resilient urban landscape.

(f) The Plastic Whale Circular Furniture Collection

- **Project Overview:** The Plastic Whale Circular Furniture Collection emerges as a beacon of innovation amidst the global challenge of plastic pollution. Spearheaded by visionary designers and environmental activists, this project harnesses the potential of recycled ocean plastic to create functional and aesthetically pleasing furniture pieces. Inspired by the urgent need to address marine debris, the collection not only serves as a tangible solution to waste management but also raises awareness about the interconnectedness of human consumption and environmental conservation. Each meticulously crafted item embodies a story of transformation, turning marine litter into symbols of sustainability and hope.

- **Design Approach:** The design approach behind The Plastic Whale Circular Furniture Collection is rooted in a circular economy model, wherein waste is repurposed and reintegrated into the production cycle. By collaborating with local communities and partnering with recycling initiatives, designers source discarded plastic from oceans and shorelines, transforming it into raw materials for furniture manufacturing. Through innovative techniques such as 3D printing and modular construction, the collection showcases the versatility and resilience of recycled plastics while pushing the boundaries of sustainable design. Moreover, an emphasis on durability and timeless aesthetics ensures that each piece not only minimizes environmental impact but also transcends trends, advocating for a shift towards conscious consumption.

- **Impact:** The Plastic Whale Circular Furniture Collection catalyzes a ripple effect of positive change, both locally and globally. On a practical level, it helps alleviate the burden of plastic pollution in marine ecosystems, mitigating harm to aquatic life and preserving fragile ecosystems. Furthermore, by transforming waste into desirable products, the collection challenges perceptions of value and waste, fostering a mindset shift towards a more circular and sustainable economy. Beyond its environmental impact, the project serves as a catalyst for community engagement and social empowerment, creating opportunities for education, employment, and advocacy. As a symbol of innovation and environmental stewardship, The Plastic Whale Circular Furniture Collection inspires individuals and industries alike to reimagine the possibilities of sustainable design and embrace a future where waste becomes a resource for regeneration.

(g) The Salvaged Ring by Bario Neal

- **Project Overview:** "The Salvaged Ring by Bario Neal" stands as a testament to the marriage of artistry and sustainability within the jewelry industry. This project represents a departure from conventional practices, where precious metals and gemstones are often sourced through environmentally damaging mining operations. Instead, Bario Neal pioneers a new paradigm by utilizing reclaimed and ethically sourced materials to craft exquisite, one of a kind rings. Rooted in the principles of environmental stewardship and social responsibility, The Salvaged Ring not only offers a symbol of love and commitment but also embodies a commitment to protecting the planet and supporting ethical labor practices.

- **Design Approach:** Bario Neal's design approach for The Salvaged Ring embodies a meticulous blend of creativity, craftsmanship, and sustainability. Each ring is meticulously crafted by skilled artisans using reclaimed precious metals and ethically sourced gemstones, ensuring minimal environmental impact and maximum social benefit. By embracing imperfections and celebrating the unique character of salvaged materials, the design process imbues each ring with a sense of authenticity and individuality. Moreover, Bario Neal fosters transparency and traceability throughout the supply chain, empowering consumers to make informed choices and championing ethical practices within the jewelry industry.

- **Impact:** The Salvaged Ring by Bario Neal extends its impact far beyond the realm of jewelry, serving as a catalyst for positive change within the luxury goods sector. By prioritizing sustainability and ethical sourcing, the project challenges industry norms and inspires other designers and brands to embrace more responsible practices. Furthermore, by supporting artisanal craftsmanship and fair labor standards, The Salvaged Ring fosters economic empowerment and social equity within local communities. Ultimately, each ring becomes a tangible symbol of conscious consumerism and a reminder of the profound connection between individuals, their choices, and the health of the planet. Through The Salvaged Ring, Bario Neal not only celebrates love but also embodies a commitment to creating a more just, equitable, and sustainable world.

(h) The Adidas x Parley Ocean Plastic Sneaker

- **Project Overview:** The Adidas x Parley Ocean Plastic Sneaker stands as a pioneering collaboration at the intersection of fashion, innovation, and environmental activism. Born from a shared commitment to combating marine plastic pollution, this project reimagines the iconic Adidas sneaker using recycled ocean plastic waste. By intercepting plastic debris from coastal regions and transforming it into high performance footwear, the collaboration not only raises awareness about the urgent need to protect our oceans but also offers a tangible solution to the global plastic crisis. Each pair of sneakers embodies a powerful message of sustainability, style, and social responsibility, inviting consumers to tread lightly and leave a positive impact with every step.

- **Design Approach:** The design approach behind the Adidas x Parley Ocean Plastic Sneaker is rooted in a holistic commitment to sustainability and performance. Collaborating with Parley for the Oceans, Adidas leverages innovative technologies to transform marine plastic waste into a high quality yarn known as Ocean Plastic®. This material serves as the foundation for the sneaker's upper, delivering both durability and breathability while reducing reliance on virgin plastic. Additionally, the design incorporates other eco-friendly elements, such as recycled polyester laces and sustainable rubber outsoles, to minimize environmental impact throughout the product's lifecycle. By prioritizing both style and sustainability, the Adidas x Parley sneaker sets a new standard for eco-conscious footwear design, inspiring consumers and industry stakeholders alike to rethink the possibilities of sustainable fashion.

- **Impact:** The Adidas x Parley Ocean Plastic Sneaker catalyzes a ripple effect of positive change across the fashion industry and beyond. By demonstrating the viability of recycled materials in high performance footwear, the collaboration encourages other brands to adopt more sustainable practices and embrace circularity in their production processes. Moreover, the project raises awareness about the interconnectedness of consumer choices and environmental conservation, inspiring individuals to reconsider their purchasing habits and support brands that prioritize sustainability. Beyond its environmental impact, the Adidas x Parley sneaker fosters collaboration and innovation within the fashion industry, driving progress towards a more sustainable and equitable future. As a symbol of innovation, style, and environmental stewardship, this collaboration exemplifies the transformative power of conscious consumerism and collective action in the fight against plastic pollution.

(i) ***The ReFlow Gypsum Concrete Collection by Taktl LLC***

- ***Project Overview:*** The ReFlow Gypsum Concrete Collection by Taktl LLC represents a bold reimagining of construction materials and practices with a focus on sustainability and circularity. Through innovative processes, this project transforms waste gypsum commonly found in construction and demolition debris into high performance architectural elements. By diverting gypsum waste from landfills and repurposing it into durable, aesthetically pleasing products, the collection not only addresses environmental concerns but also offers a practical solution for the construction industry. Each piece in the ReFlow Collection embodies a commitment to resource efficiency, durability, and design excellence, paving the way for a more sustainable future in architecture and design.

- ***Design Approach:*** Taktl LLC's design approach for the ReFlow Gypsum Concrete Collection is rooted in a comprehensive understanding of material science, craftsmanship, and sustainability principles. Through a proprietary process, waste gypsum is transformed into a versatile material that can be molded into various architectural elements, including panels, tiles, and countertops. The design process prioritizes durability, versatility, and aesthetic appeal, ensuring that each product meets the highest standards of quality and performance. Moreover, by incorporating recycled content and minimizing waste throughout the manufacturing process, Taktl LLC minimizes environmental impact while maximizing resource efficiency. Through collaboration with architects, designers, and builders, the ReFlow Collection offers a customizable solution for sustainable interior and exterior applications, enabling creative expression without compromising on environmental responsibility.

- ***Impact:*** The ReFlow Gypsum Concrete Collection by Taktl LLC has a far reaching impact on the construction industry, sustainability practices, and environmental conservation efforts. By repurposing waste gypsum into durable architectural elements, the project reduces the demand for virgin materials and diverts construction and demolition debris from landfills, thus mitigating environmental harm and conserving valuable resources. Furthermore, the collection serves as a catalyst for innovation and collaboration within the design and construction sectors, inspiring stakeholders to rethink traditional approaches and embrace sustainable alternatives. As architects, designers, and builders integrate the ReFlow Collection into their projects, they contribute to a more sustainable built environment and promote a culture of responsible consumption and production. Ultimately, the ReFlow Gypsum Concrete Collection exemplifies the transformative power of circular design, demonstrating how waste can be turned into opportunity, and sustainability can be seamlessly integrated into every aspect of the built environment.

These case studies illustrate the diverse applications of recycled materials in design projects, showcasing the innovative use of waste materials to create functional, aesthetic, and sustainable products. By harnessing the creative potential of recycled materials, designers can contribute to the circular economy, reduce resource consumption, and promote environmental stewardship in the design industry.

14.3 Consideration of Lifecycle Analysis and Carbon Footprint in Design Products

In today's environmentally conscious world, it's imperative for designers to consider the lifecycle analysis (LCA) and carbon footprint of their products. Understanding the environmental impact of design decisions throughout a product's lifecycle, from raw material extraction to disposal, is essential for promoting sustainability and reducing ecological harm. Here's an exploration of how LCA and carbon footprint considerations influence design practices:

(a) Lifecycle Analysis (LCA)

Lifecycle analysis, also known as life cycle assessment, is a methodology used to evaluate the environmental impacts of a product or service throughout its entire lifecycle. This comprehensive approach considers all stages of the product lifecycle, including raw material extraction, manufacturing, distribution, use, and end of life disposal. By quantifying the environmental inputs and outputs associated with each stage, designers can identify opportunities to minimize resource consumption, reduce waste generation, and mitigate environmental pollution.

(b) Carbon Footprint

The carbon footprint of a product refers to the total amount of greenhouse gas emissions, typically measured in carbon dioxide equivalent (CO_2e), generated over its lifecycle. This includes emissions associated with energy consumption, transportation, manufacturing processes, and end of life disposal. Designers aim to minimize the carbon footprint of their products by optimizing energy efficiency, reducing fossil fuel consumption, and incorporating renewable energy sources into manufacturing processes.

(c) Design Considerations

When designing products with sustainability in mind, designers consider a range of factors to minimize environmental impact and promote resource efficiency. This includes selecting low impact materials, optimizing product durability and longevity, designing for disassembly and recyclability, and reducing energy consumption during manufacturing and use. By incorporating these considerations into the design process, designers can create products that are environmentally responsible and socially beneficial.

(d) Material Selection

The choice of materials has a significant impact on the environmental footprint of a product. Designers prioritize the use of sustainable materials, such as recycled content, renewable resources, and biodegradable materials, to minimize resource depletion and reduce pollution. Additionally, designers consider the embodied energy and carbon emissions associated with different materials, selecting options with lower environmental impact wherever possible.

(e) Manufacturing Processes

The manufacturing phase of a product's lifecycle is a critical stage where designers can influence environmental impact. Designers strive to optimize manufacturing processes to minimize energy consumption, reduce waste generation, and eliminate hazardous substances. This may involve adopting lean manufacturing principles, implementing closed loop systems for material recycling, and integrating renewable energy sources into production facilities.

(f) Transportation and Distribution

Transportation and distribution logistics contribute to the carbon footprint of a product by consuming fossil fuels and emitting greenhouse gases. Designers seek to minimize transportation distances and optimize supply chain efficiency to reduce emissions associated with product distribution. This may involve sourcing materials locally, consolidating shipments, and utilizing sustainable transportation modes such as rail or sea freight.

(g) Product Use and Maintenance

The use phase of a product's lifecycle represents another opportunity for designers to promote sustainability. Designers develop products that are energy efficient, easy to maintain, and durable, encouraging users to prolong product lifespan and minimize resource consumption. Additionally, designers provide clear instructions for product maintenance and repair, empowering users to extend product usability and reduce the need for premature replacement.

(h) End of Life Disposal

Proper disposal and end of life management are essential considerations in designing sustainable products. Designers prioritize recyclability, biodegradability, and compostability to facilitate the responsible disposal of products at the end of their lifecycle. Additionally, designers explore circular economy principles such as product take back programs and materials recovery initiatives to minimize waste generation and promote resource recovery.

In a nutshell, lifecycle analysis and carbon footprint considerations are integral to designing sustainable products that minimize environmental impact and promote resource efficiency. By adopting a holistic approach to design that considers the entire product lifecycle, designers can create innovative solutions that meet user needs while safeguarding the health of the planet for future generations.

15

Minimizing Environmental Impact

In this concluding chapter, "Minimizing Environmental Impact," the journey towards sustainability reaches its apex as readers are empowered with actionable insights and strategies to reduce their environmental footprint. Drawing upon the wealth of knowledge and inspiration gleaned from preceding chapters, this section serves as a call to action, urging individuals, businesses, and policymakers to embrace a collective responsibility towards the planet. From simple lifestyle changes to systemic reforms, each recommendation is imbued with the potential to catalyze positive change and shape a more resilient and equitable future for generations to come. As the curtain falls on this transformative odyssey, the message resounds loud and clear: by embracing innovation, fostering collaboration, and championing sustainability in every facet of life, we possess the power to minimize our environmental impact and forge a path towards a more harmonious coexistence with the natural world.

15.1 Strategies for Reducing the Environmental Impact of Design Projects

Designers play a pivotal role in minimizing the environmental impact of design projects by adopting sustainable practices and making conscious decisions throughout the design process. Here are several strategies for reducing the environmental footprint of design projects:

(a) Design for Durability and Longevity

One of the most effective ways to minimize environmental impact is to design products, buildings, and infrastructure with durability and longevity in mind. By prioritizing quality materials, robust construction techniques, and timeless design aesthetics, designers can create solutions that withstand the test of time, reducing the need for frequent replacements and minimizing waste generation.

(b) Optimize Material Selection

Material selection has a significant impact on the environmental footprint of design projects. Designers should prioritize the use of sustainable materials, such as recycled content, rapidly renewable resources, and low impact alternatives, to minimize resource depletion and pollution. Additionally, designers should consider the embodied energy and carbon emissions associated with different materials, selecting options with lower environmental impact wherever possible.

(c) Embrace Circular Design Principles

Circular design principles aim to minimize waste and maximize resource efficiency by designing products and systems with closed loop lifecycles. Designers can adopt circular design strategies such as designing for disassembly, reuse, remanufacturing, and recycling to extend product lifespan and facilitate material recovery at the end of life. By embracing circularity, designers can contribute to a more sustainable and regenerative economy.

(d) Reduce Energy Consumption

Energy consumption is a significant contributor to the environmental footprint of design projects. Designers should prioritize energy efficient design solutions, such as passive heating and cooling strategies, daylighting, and high performance building envelopes, to minimize energy demand and reduce greenhouse gas emissions. Additionally, designers should integrate renewable energy sources, such as solar, wind, and geothermal, into project designs to further reduce reliance on fossil fuels.

(e) Minimize Waste Generation

Waste generation is a key environmental concern in design projects, particularly in construction and manufacturing processes. Designers should adopt waste reduction strategies, such as lean manufacturing principles, material optimization techniques, and construction waste management plans, to minimize waste generation and promote resource efficiency throughout the project lifecycle. Additionally, designers should explore opportunities for upcycling and repurposing waste materials to minimize landfilling and promote circularity.

(f) Optimize Transportation and Logistics

Transportation and logistics contribute to the environmental footprint of design projects through fuel consumption and emissions. Designers should prioritize local sourcing of materials, components, and labor to minimize transportation distances and reduce carbon emissions associated with product distribution. Additionally, designers should explore sustainable transportation modes, such as rail or sea freight, and consolidate shipments to further reduce environmental impact.

(g) Promote Biodiversity and Ecosystem Health

Design projects have the potential to impact biodiversity and ecosystem health through habitat destruction, pollution, and resource extraction. Designers should prioritize the preservation and restoration of natural ecosystems, incorporating green infrastructure, sustainable landscaping, and biodiversity friendly design elements into project designs. By promoting biodiversity and ecosystem health, designers can contribute to the resilience and sustainability of the built environment.

(h) Engage Stakeholders and Communities

Collaboration and engagement with stakeholders and communities are essential for designing sustainable solutions that meet the needs and aspirations of diverse populations. Designers should involve stakeholders in the design process, seeking input, feedback, and co-creation opportunities to ensure that projects are socially inclusive, culturally sensitive, and environmentally responsible. By fostering dialogue and collaboration, designers can build consensus, generate innovative ideas, and create solutions that benefit both people and the planet.

By implementing these strategies and embracing sustainable design principles, designers can minimize the environmental impact of design projects and contribute to a more sustainable and resilient built environment. Through creativity, innovation, and collaboration, designers have the power to address pressing environmental challenges and create solutions that enhance quality of life while safeguarding the health of the planet for future generations.

15.2 Discussion on the Role of Designers in Promoting Sustainability and Conservation

As, discussed in the previous section, designers role in promoting sustainability and conservation through their creative endeavours and decision making processes is a key role. As champions of innovation and problem solving, designers have the unique opportunity to influence the environmental impact of products, services, and built environments. Here, we explore the multifaceted role of designers in promoting sustainability and conservation:

(a) Redefining Norms and Standards

Designers have the power to challenge existing norms and standards by redefining what constitutes good design. By advocating for sustainability principles and incorporating environmental considerations into design criteria, designers can help shift industry practices towards more sustainable and conservation oriented approaches. This includes promoting the use of eco-friendly materials, reducing energy consumption, and minimizing waste generation throughout the product lifecycle.

(b) Educating and Raising Awareness

Designers can serve as educators and advocates for sustainability by raising awareness about environmental issues and promoting eco-conscious behavior among stakeholders and consumers. Through their work, designers can communicate complex environmental concepts in accessible and engaging ways, encouraging people to make informed choices that minimize their ecological footprint. Designers can also leverage their platforms to highlight the importance of conservation efforts and inspire action towards a more sustainable future.

(c) Fostering Innovation and Collaboration

Sustainability challenges require innovative solutions that go beyond traditional design approaches. Designers can drive innovation by collaborating with scientists, engineers, policymakers, and other stakeholders to develop sustainable technologies, systems, and practices. By fostering interdisciplinary collaboration and knowledge exchange, designers can harness the collective expertise and creativity of diverse stakeholders to address complex environmental problems and drive positive change.

(d) Advocating for Policy Change

Designers can advocate for policy change at local, national, and international levels to support sustainability and conservation goals. By engaging with policymakers, industry leaders, and advocacy groups, designers can influence the development of regulations, standards, and incentives that promote sustainable design practices and environmental stewardship. Designers can also use their expertise to inform policy debates and contribute to the formulation of evidence based solutions to pressing environmental challenges.

(e) Leading by Example

Designers have the opportunity to lead by example by integrating sustainability principles into their own design practices and projects. By adopting sustainable design strategies, such as life cycle assessment, biomimicry, and design for disassembly, designers can demonstrate the feasibility and benefits of environmentally conscious design approaches. Through showcase projects and case studies, designers can inspire their peers and clients to embrace sustainability as a core value and design criterion.

(f) Empowering Communities

Designers can empower communities to take ownership of their environmental destiny by involving them in the design process and co-creating solutions that address their unique needs and aspirations. By fostering participatory design processes and community engagement initiatives, designers can build trust, foster collaboration, and empower communities to implement sustainable practices and conservation initiatives that enhance resilience and well being.

(g) Promoting Ethical Consumption

Designers have a responsibility to consider the social and environmental impacts of the products and services they create and promote ethical consumption habits among consumers. By designing products that are durable, repairable, and recyclable, designers can encourage responsible consumption patterns and reduce resource consumption and waste generation. Designers can also advocate for transparency and accountability in supply chains, helping consumers make informed choices that align with their values and support sustainability goals.

A designer's role is very significant in promoting sustainability and conservation by reimagining design practices, raising awareness, fostering innovation, advocating for policy change, leading by example, empowering communities, and promoting ethical consumption. Through their creative vision, collaborative spirit, and commitment to positive change, designers can contribute to building a more sustainable and resilient future for people and the planet.

15.3 Consideration of the Circular Economy and Cradle-to-Cradle Design Principles

In the quest for sustainability, the concepts of the circular economy and cradle-to-cradle design principles have emerged as powerful frameworks for rethinking how we produce, consume, and dispose of goods. Designers play a critical role in applying these principles to create products and systems that minimize waste, maximize resource efficiency, and promote environmental regeneration. Let's delve into the considerations of these two approaches:

(a) Circular Economy

The circular economy is a regenerative economic model that aims to decouple economic growth from resource consumption and environmental degradation. At its core, the circular economy seeks to keep resources in use for as long as possible, extract maximum value from them during their lifecycle, and recover and regenerate materials at the end of their service life. Designers play a pivotal role in the circular economy by designing products, services, and systems that are restorative and regenerative rather than linear and wasteful.

Key Principles of the Circular Economy:

- *Design for Durability and Longevity:* Designers can extend the lifespan of products by prioritizing durability, reparability, and upgradability. By designing products that last longer and require less frequent replacement, designers can reduce resource consumption and waste generation over time.

- *Design for Reuse and Repurposing:* Designers can design products with modular components and standardized interfaces that facilitate disassembly, repair, and reuse. By enabling products to be easily disassembled and reconfigured for new uses, designers can extend their lifecycle and minimize the need for virgin materials.

- *Design for Material Circularity:* Designers can prioritize the use of renewable, biodegradable, and recyclable materials in their designs, as well as incorporating recycled content and designing for recyclability. By designing products with materials that can be easily recovered and regenerated at the end of their service life, designers can close the loop and minimize the extraction of finite resources.

- *Design for Waste Elimination:* Designers can adopt strategies to minimize waste generation throughout the product lifecycle, such as designing with minimal packaging, reducing excess material usage, and optimizing production processes for efficiency. By eliminating waste at the source, designers can reduce environmental pollution and conserve natural resources.

(b) Cradle-to-Cradle Design Principles

Cradle-to-cradle design principles are based on the idea that waste should be eliminated from the design process entirely, and products should be designed to be inherently restorative and regenerative. Cradle-to-cradle design seeks to mimic natural systems by ensuring that materials and nutrients are continuously circulated and replenished, rather than being disposed of as waste. Designers can apply cradle-to-cradle principles to create products that are safe, healthy, and beneficial for both people and the environment.

Key Principles of Cradle-to-Cradle Design:

- *Material Health:* Designers should prioritize the use of materials that are safe, non-toxic, and biodegradable, avoiding harmful chemicals and pollutants that can harm human health and the environment. By selecting materials that are inherently safe and healthy, designers can create products that contribute to a more sustainable and equitable world.

- *Material Reutilization:* Designers should design products with materials that can be easily recovered, recycled, and reused in continuous cycles of regeneration. By designing products with materials that can be perpetually cycled through the economy without losing quality or value, designers can minimize the need for virgin resources and reduce environmental impact.

- *Renewable Energy:* Designers should prioritize the use of renewable energy sources in the production and operation of products, reducing reliance on fossil fuels and minimizing greenhouse gas emissions. By harnessing the power of renewable energy technologies such as solar, wind, and hydroelectric power, designers can create products that are more sustainable, resilient, and energy efficient.

- *Water Stewardship:* Designers should design products and systems that minimize water consumption, pollution, and waste, promoting efficient use and conservation of this vital resource. By incorporating water saving technologies, reusing wastewater, and protecting natural water systems, designers can contribute to the sustainable management of water resources and the protection of aquatic ecosystems.

In conclusion, the circular economy and cradle-to-cradle design principles offer powerful frameworks for promoting sustainability and conservation in design practice. By embracing these principles and integrating them into their design processes, designers can create products and systems that are restorative, regenerative, and resilient, contributing to a more sustainable and equitable future for generations to come.

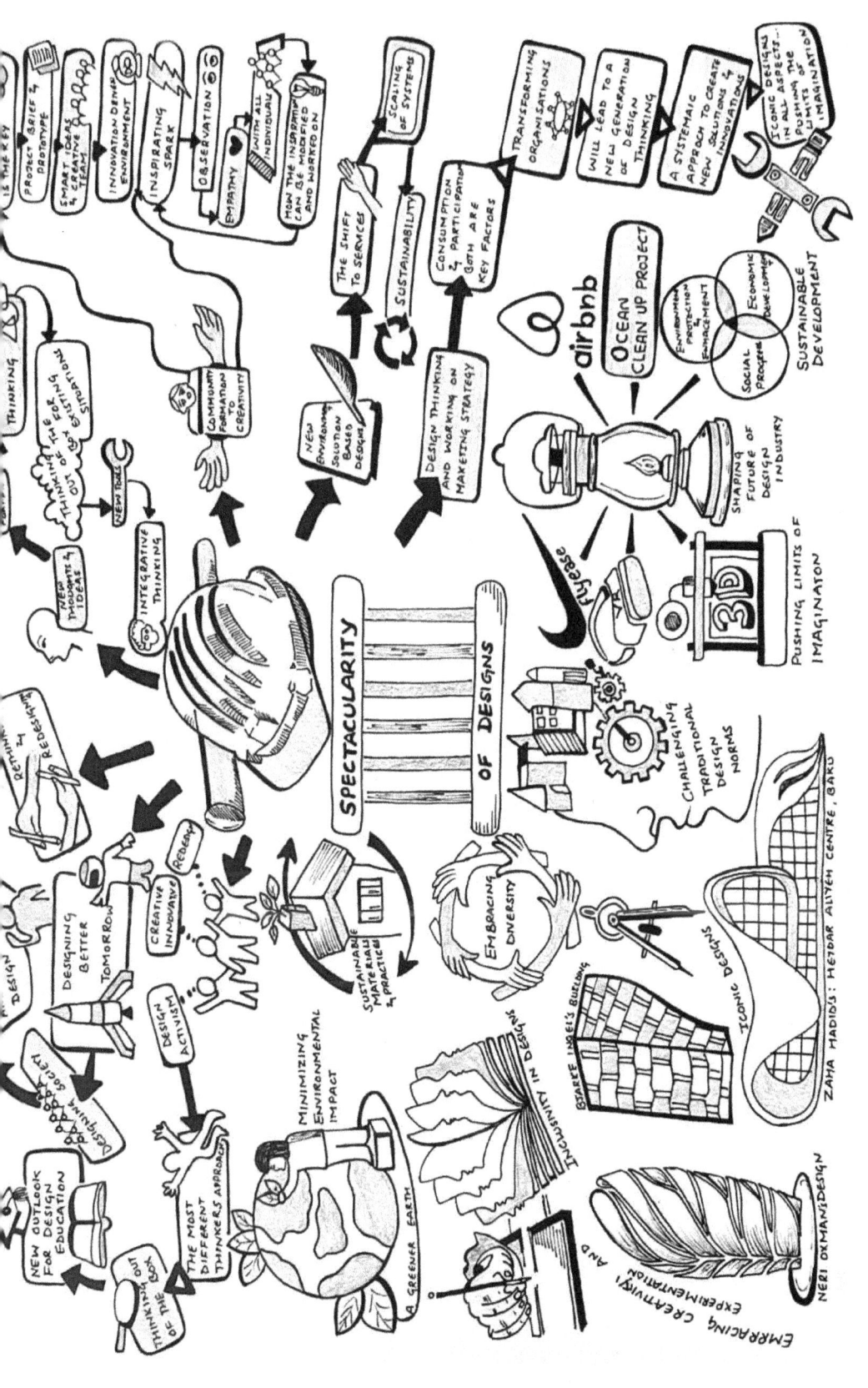

www.ingramcontent.com/pod-product-compliance
Lightning Source LLC
LaVergne TN
LVHW061551070526
838199LV00077B/6998